Interpreting Slavery with Children and Teens at Museums and Historic Sites

AMERICAN ASSOCIATION *for* **STATE** *and* **LOCAL HISTORY**

About the Organization

The American Association for State and Local History (AASLH) is a national history membership association headquartered in Nashville, Tennessee, that provides leadership and support for its members who preserve and interpret state and local history in order to make the past more meaningful to all people. AASLH members are leaders in preserving, researching, and interpreting traces of the American past to connect the people, thoughts, and events of yesterday with the creative memories and abiding concerns of people, communities, and our nation today. In addition to sponsorship of this book series, AASLH publishes History News magazine, a newsletter, technical leaflets and reports, and other materials; confers prizes and awards in recognition of outstanding achievement in the field; supports a broad education program and other activities designed to help members work more effectively; and advocates on behalf of the discipline of history. To join AASLH, go to www.aaslh.org or contact Membership Services, AASLH, 2021 21st Ave. South, Suite 320, Nashville, TN 37212.

About the Series

The American Association for State and Local History publishes the *Interpreting History* series in order to provide expert, in-depth guidance in interpretation for history professionals at museums and historic sites. The books are intended to help practitioners expand their interpretation to be more inclusive of the range of American history.

Books in this series help readers:

- quickly learn about the questions surrounding a specific topic,
- introduce them to the challenges of interpreting this part of history, and
- highlight best practice examples of how interpretation has been done by different organizations.

They enable institutions to place their interpretative efforts into a larger context, despite each having a specific and often localized mission. These books serve as quick references to practical considerations, further research, and historical information.

Titles in the Series

Interpreting Slavery with Children and Teens at Museums and Historic Sites

Kristin L. Gallas

ROWMAN & LITTLEFIELD
Lanham • Boulder • New York • London

Published by Rowman & Littlefield

An imprint of The Rowman & Littlefield Publishing Group, Inc.

4501 Forbes Boulevard, Suite 200, Lanham, Maryland 20706

www.rowman.com

6 Tinworth Street, London SE11 5AL, United Kingdom

British Library Cataloguing in Publication Information Available

Library of Congress Cataloging-in-Publication Data

Names: Gallas, Kris, author.

Title: Interpreting slavery with children and teens at museums and historic sites / Kristin L. Gallas.

Description: Lanham : Rowman & Littlefield, [2021] | Series: Interpreting history | Includes bibliographical references and index.

Identifiers: LCCN 2021019543 (print) | LCCN 2021019544 (ebook) | ISBN 9781538100691 (cloth) | ISBN 9781538100707 (paperback) | ISBN 9781538100714 (ebook)

Subjects: LCSH: Slavery in museum exhibits—United States. | Historic sites—Interpretive programs—United States. | Slavery—United States—Historiography. | Museums—Educational aspects—United States. | Museums and children—United States.

Classification: LCC AM7 .G335 2021 (print) | LCC AM7 (ebook) | DDC 306.3/6207473—dc23

LC record available at https://lccn.loc.gov/2021019543

LC ebook record available at https://lccn.loc.gov/2021019544

To my colleagues in the museum, historic site, and public history field:

Thank you for doing this important work, for giving voice to the long-silenced millions, for being respectful facilitators of student learning, and for being supportive of each other on this journey.

Remember, "Not everything that is faced can be changed; but nothing can be changed until it is faced." ~ James Baldwin

Contents

Foreword

HASAN KWAME JEFFRIES

I had an idea.

For several years I had been collaborating with the Southern Poverty Law Center's Teaching Tolerance division on projects designed to help K–12 educators teach the history of American slavery accurately and effectively. Out of these efforts sprang a detailed framework for teaching American history that included a bank of primary sources and sample units, and the *Teaching Hard History: American Slavery* podcast. Talking with educators who used the framework and listened to the podcast underscored the deep desire of teachers at all grade levels to provide students with the best possible understanding of American slavery.

The idea that began percolating in my brain was simple. Drawing on my experience with Teaching Tolerance, I reached out to colleagues affiliated with the Global Arts and Humanities Discovery Theme at Ohio State University, where I teach in the Department of History, and proposed bringing to campus twenty and odd elementary, middle, and high school teachers from Central Ohio for a four-day institute on understanding and teaching American slavery in June 2020. The institute would provide participants with detailed overviews of essential content, offer practical strategies for teaching, identify and explain the best ways to use key source material, and present proven techniques for engaging and exciting students.

I wanted elementary, middle, and high school teachers to be a part of the institute because teaching slavery effectively requires introducing the subject to students early in their educational journey and complicating their understanding of it as they mature. I also wanted teachers who specialize in a range of arts and humanities subjects to be included because slavery is best learned across the curriculum, rather than in isolated subject areas.

I proposed bringing to campus leading scholars of American slavery, including Edward Baptist, author of *The Half Has Never Been Told: Slavery and the Making of American Capitalism*, and experts on teaching slavery, such as Bethany Jay, coeditor of *Understanding and Teaching American Slavery*. Recognizing too the pivotal role that museums and historic sites play in teaching American slavery, I invited Christian Cotz, formerly the director of Education and Visitor Engagement at James Madison's Montpelier in Orange, Virginia, to lead a workshop. I also planned a daylong trip to the National Underground Railroad and Freedom Center in Cincinnati, Ohio.

I was excited about the possibilities of the summer institute, and my colleagues, who enthusiastically endorsed the project, were too. But before the dean of the College of Arts and Sciences could approve the necessary funding, the coronavirus hit, shutting down the university. There would be no institute, or so I thought.

As summer neared, the dean reached out, inquiring about the possibility of holding the institute virtually. "This could work," I thought, but not as a stand-alone online convening, but rather as a yearlong series of webinars culminating in three days of in-person workshops in June 2021. The dean approved funding for the reconfigured institute, which began with two webinars in summer 2020, the first on pedagogical techniques for teaching slavery remotely, and the second on using the *Freedom on the Move* digital database of fugitive slave advertisements. There were two additional webinars in fall 2020, one on slavery during the colonial era, and the other on slavery and the Constitution.

Christian Cotz led the last webinar. For two hours, he shared invaluable insights regarding lessons learned from developing and displaying *A Mere Distinction of Colour*, a permanent exhibition on slavery in America and at Madison's plantation estate that opened at James Madison's Montpelier in 2017. And after he was done, he spent another hour with us as we discussed the tense teaching environment that many have found themselves working in as a result of politically charged animus directed at those teaching the hard history of American slavery.

One of the teachers who talked candidly about this challenge was Justin Emrich, a brilliant young educator who teaches eighth-grade social studies in a nearly all-white suburban school district just north of Columbus, Ohio. Justin explained that at the beginning of the school year he placed cardboard cutouts of a couple of notable historical and contemporary figures, including basketball superstar Lebron James, in classroom seats left vacant because of distance learning. But as soon as the district posted an image of the cutouts on its Facebook page, his principal received emails from parents complaining about political bias. When asked to explain himself, Justin said, "I looked at my boss and I said, 'They don't get to win anymore.' Those voices that we've always let dictate our policy to us, they don't get to win anymore. We're on the right side of this."

In addition to participating in the teaching institute, Justin had spent the summer marching alongside students during the Black Lives Matter protests that had swept across the country and leading a reading group for former students on anti-racism. Reflecting on these experiences, Justin was sure that teaching American slavery honestly was "the right thing." In the past, he said, "I've been scared of the pushback. Now I almost relish it. Tell me why being anti-racist is wrong. I'll wait."

Justin had the truth of it. Embracing anti-racist pedagogy, which includes teaching American slavery forthrightly, is the right thing to do. To do anything less is to contribute to the miseducation of yet another generation of young people.

I had an idea.

I wanted to develop an institute to help a handful of Ohio educators like Justin teach their students the truth about American slavery. If I am lucky, I will reach a couple dozen teachers over the next two years and, indirectly, a couple thousand students. That is no small thing, but it also speaks to the limited reach of classroom instruction.

This is why I am so glad Kristin Gallas had an idea too. She wanted to help museums and historic sites extend the work of classroom educators like Justin by embracing practices and developing programs for school-age children and their families that would provide an unvarnished look at American slavery.

Gallas's idea, which is now this book, has the potential to transform the way the public understands American slavery. But to do so, public history professionals, when they pick up this book, have to muster the courage to implement what's inside.

For far too long, those who have popularized a sanitized version of American slavery, narratives that decenter Black experiences and gloss over slavery's centrality to this nation's birth and growth, have won the day. But they don't get to win anymore. From this moment forward, the truth wins.

Acknowledgments

Many people have been a part of the four-year journey to write this book. Each person deserves my utmost gratitude and appreciation for their help. Special thanks go to my frequent collaborator James DeWolf Perry, who was a sounding board for the development of this project and helped to shape the initial chapters. To my friend, colleague, and teacher Nicole Moore, your comments on the manuscript were invaluable and provided much needed levity and grounding during the final phase of the writing. To Dr. Bob Beatty, your edits were the finishing touch the manuscript needed. And, to my dear friend Patricia Brooks, you were one of the first people I met on this journey, and I am ever grateful for your friendship and guidance.

I would like to extend my gratitude to the museums and historic sites that permitted me to observe programs as part of my research.

- Frederick Douglass National Historic Site—Nate Johnson
- Historic London Town—Kristen Butler
- Moffatt-Ladd House—Barbara Ward, Jennifer Belmont-Earl, and Keith Mascoll
- Mount Vernon—Linda Powell, Jessie MacLeod, and Allison Wickens
- President Lincoln's Cottage—Callie Hawkins
- Royall House and Slave Quarters—Amy Peters Clark, Gracelaw Simmons, and Penny Outlaw

Thank you to my colleagues who shared their professional knowledge and experiences through interviews and emails:

- Jeff Boorom—Fort Snelling
- Elon Cook Lee—public historian and consultant
- Richard Cooper—Conner Prairie
- Christian Cotz and Kyle Stetz—Montpelier
- Emmanuel Dabney—Petersburg National Battlefield
- Dr. Jon-Paul Dyson—Strong Museum of Play
- Candra Flanagan, Anna Hindley, and Jennifer Zazo-Brown—National Museum of African American History and Culture
- Conny Graft—Conny Graft Research and Evaluation
- Linnea Grim and Brandon Dillard—Monticello
- Dr. Sheila Kirschbaum—Tsongas Industrial History Center
- Sarah Jencks and David McKenzie—Ford's Theatre Society

- Andrea Jones—Peak Experiences Lab
- Richard Josey—Collective Journeys
- Dr. Mariruth Leftwich and Amanda McAllen—Heinz History Center
- Shannon Moeck—Cedar Creek/Belle Grove National Historic Site
- Sarah Pharon, Bradon Paynter—International Coalition of Sites of Conscience
- Dr. Julia Rose—Marietta House Museum, M-NCPPC, Department of Parks and Recreation, Prince George's County
- The leadership team at Salem Maritime National Historic Site
- Dr. Amy Tyson—DePaul University

To my parents—Donna and Michael—who encouraged my love of history. For my niece, Brianne, your drive to make the world a just, equitable, and loving place assures me that the future is in good hands. To Yasmine, for making my vision of the braid graphic come to life. And, to Darryl, my love. Thank you for dancing with me through the joyful times and supporting me through the tough times. You help me see the world from a different perspective, and I could not ask for a better teacher and partner.

Preface

"Slavery was not a sideshow in American history. It was the main event." —Glenn Collins[1]

Presenting the history of slavery to young people in a comprehensive and conscientious manner *is* difficult and necessitates challenging the prevailing and incomplete narrative and our tried-and-true interpretive techniques. It requires diligence and compassion—for the history itself, for those telling the story, and for those hearing the stories. The history of African chattel slavery in the United States is a necessary part of the collective narrative about our past, present, and future. A comprehensive narrative of slavery defies centuries of status-quo white supremacy in this country. We cannot continue to drape our history in a shroud of silence, coded mythology, and dog whistles. Dr. Andre Perry, senior fellow at the Brookings Institution, states, "The future of our democracy depends upon youth's understanding of our past. Teaching slavery isn't about airing dirty laundry. It's about baring the hidden roots of racism, the source of injustice in our modern-day society."[2] We must talk *with* young people about slavery and race, as it is not enough to just talk *to* them or *about* the subject.

The book's title, *Interpreting Slavery with Children and Teens at Museums and Historic Sites*, uses the preposition "with" for just that reason. By engaging students in dialogue about slavery, they bring their prior knowledge, scaffold new knowledge, and create their own relevance—all while adults *hear* them and show respect for what they have to say. For that reason, this book specifically addresses interpersonal tours, programs, and activities for youth, with some notes about applying the theory and practice to family programs.[3] Talking with students can begin to break the cycle, as evidenced by an encounter historical interpreter Dontavius Williams had with a fifth grader at Historic Brattonsville in 2012.

> While at the slave cabin, one of my coworkers was describing the building and those who lived in it; a little boy starts talking to his friend (who appears to be mixed) and says, "Man I wish I had slaves now . . . that way I could get them to do all my work for me for free." Immediately, a nerve was struck. I called the little boy over to me and quietly attempted to redirect his thinking. To no avail. It is a sad truth that there is still a small segment of America that still has this mentality. Whether it was a joke, him trying to be cute in front of his friends, or just seeking attention wherever it could be found, the comment was and still is unacceptable. His one comment made me think, "Is this what he is being taught at home?" This is the reason why sites like ours exist. We *must* continue to educate our children because if we don't, we face the risk of falling back into what held so many of our ancestors in bondage.[4]

We cannot fail future generations of learners the way many of us were failed by the adults in our lives.

The history of slavery and racism are inextricably linked. We cannot talk about one without the other. From 1640—the first incident of an African man, John Punch, being forced to "serve his said master or his assigns for the time of his natural life here or elsewhere"—to the very end of slavery in 1865, when Billy McCrea, Harriet Smith, and thousands of other enslaved people were emancipated in Texas, being Black in North America (the colonies and subsequently the United States) meant living under the shadow of enslavement.[5] In the ensuing one hundred and fifty-plus years, being Black in North America has meant being under the shadow of Jim Crow, systemic racism, and discrimination. A patchwork of laws, amendments, acts, and court cases have attempted to undo the biases that are ingrained in the fiber of everyday life in the United States. In 1967, President Lyndon B. Johnson commissioned the "Report of the National Advisory Commission on Civil Disorders," known as the Kerner Commission, to investigate racial unrest that plagued the country that summer. The report's findings, which Johnson and subsequent administrations largely ignored, still ring eerily true in the summer of 2020.

> Segregation and poverty have created in the racial ghetto a destructive environment totally unknown to most white Americans. What white Americans have never fully understood—but what the Negro can never forget—is that white society is deeply implicated in the ghetto. White institutions created it, white institutions maintain it, and white society condones it.[6]

White people created and maintained the institution of chattel slavery in the United States, and today most white Americans live their lives completely disconnected from its legacies. Learning about slavery is not about placing blame, guilt, or shame. Educating one's self about slavery and its legacies is to better understand the state of the United States today. And what better place to help young Americans learn about the relevance of our collective history than museums and historic sites. As Williams noted, that is why we exist.

Notes on Language:

Throughout the book, I chose to use the term "enslaved" to describe the people held in the bondage of chattel slavery. The term "slave" appears only in quoted historical documents or secondary sources. I use the word "slavery" to describe the institution, as it is a historical term that immediately invokes both the evil and agency of the institution. In some places, I have used the more contemporary term "enslavement" to refer to the multi-generational bondage of African-descended people.

Knowing that each institution employs a different title for similar jobs, I used, interchangeably, the terms educator, museum educator, interpreter, and tour guide to refer to staff members and volunteers who develop and conduct school programs at museums and historic sites.

Why Me?

I came to this work in 2009 when Katrina Browne hired me to educate teachers and museum professionals on the history and legacies of slavery in conjunction with the release of her film *Traces of the Trade: A Story from the Deep North*. I had a background in formal and informal learning and a passion for sharing the stories of historically marginalized groups, but I had never done any intensive work on my own biases or connections with the institution of slavery. Having been raised as a white, middle-class, cis-gender female in suburban Vermont, whose ancestors were *Mayflower* passengers on one side and southern European immigrants on the other, race was not a conscious part of my everyday existence. There was one student in my high school who identified as Black, and four Vietnamese siblings from a refugee family. This was the extent of our "racial" diversity.

Until I moved to Montana and worked with members of indigenous tribes, I had never encountered anyone significantly different from me. A subsequent move to Boston exposed me to people and resources that helped me explore my identity and relationship to bias and racism. It also put me in a position to examine how the public history field was (or was not) interpreting African American history. Later, an ancestry search turned up a Puritan forefather who bequeathed "a negro girl, aged about eighteen" to his daughters. There, I found it—a slave-holding ancestor, from Massachusetts no less. I had a familial connection to the institution of slavery.

I am still reckoning with what it means to be white in the United States. Through the process of learning about the extent of the institution of slavery in the country and examining my own racial biases, I have been able to open avenues for myself and others to examine our relationship to race and to act more deliberately when developing programs on the history of slavery.

No matter how many Black friends I have, or how much knowledge I have about the history and pedagogy, I needed to recognize, and continue to recognize, my shortcomings in this field. I will never know what it is like to be descended from enslaved people or to be a Black person in the twenty-first-century United States. While working on an exhibit about the history of free Black sailors on the USS *Constitution*, I visited with the African American priest at a friend's Catholic church. I confessed to Father Pratt that I felt inadequate about telling the story of Black sailors. I was anxious and felt like an imposter. He assured me that the work was important, and that in my professional position I was charged with telling a very important story. He said that I had a responsibility to tell the story. His pep talk—which I can only believe was sincere coming from a priest—gave me the boost I needed to see my role as a white person in this field. I am not the only voice, but one of many in a choir helping to center the voices of the enslaved, illuminate a comprehensive historical narrative, and highlight slavery's legacies in our world today.

I do not have all the answers, but I ask a lot of questions and am willing to listen. For public historians, especially those of us who are white, these acknowledgements are hard, but extremely important. We must wrestle with our own biases and identities. We must be knowledgeable and humble, sharing authority with our colleagues, community stakeholders, and our student visitors.

The Work Continues

In *Interpreting Slavery at Museums and Historic Sites* (2014), my colleague James DeWolf Perry and I developed a framework that historic sites and museums can use to help structure the development of a comprehensive and conscientious interpretation of slavery.[7] The book includes chapters by leaders in this field providing lessons learned and replicable practices. The framework's six categories—comprehensive content, race and identity awareness, institutional investment, community involvement, visitor experiences and expectations, and staff training—cover a broad range of theory and practices that historic sites and museums can use as a foundation for the work with young audiences outlined here.

While we were promoting the first book and conducting workshops at historic sites, colleagues kept asking us how the theory and practice outlined in *Interpreting Slavery* applied to student programs. It seemed obvious to us that many of the concepts were transferable, but upon further reflection and examination, we realized that young audiences required a more nuanced approach to program development and implementation. Those discussions prompted the research and writing of this book. Here I offer a framework, including advice, examples, and replicable practices, for the comprehensive development and implementation of slavery-related school programs at museums and historic sites. The voice of the book is intentionally informal, as I want it to be part of a conversation—a field-wide conversation between me and you, my colleagues. I pulled information from the existing literature, research from related fields, consultations with colleagues, and observations of school programs at a variety of museums and historic sites. From this research emerged a framework that has helped define the process of creating interpretive programs for young people.[8] This framework provides structure for the following chapters, and a guide for proceeding with your work. (See figure 0.1.)

Race, Identity, and Historical Trauma

Interpreting the history of slavery often requires offering students new historical narratives and helping them to navigate the emotions that arise when new narratives conflict with longstanding beliefs. The racial identity of both staff and student visitors plays a role in how we offer interpretation and how they receive it. As professionals, we must be aware of, and confident with, our own knowledge and feelings about race and slavery. We must also understand where students are coming from to help them better understand their own concerns surrounding race and identity when learning about slavery.

The traumatic nature of this history sits both at the surface and is buried deep in the souls of Black Americans who descend from enslaved people. We must be aware that it is a distinct possibility that we could be traumatizing or retraumatizing students with this history, so we must take steps to ensure their emotional and psychological care, while also being cognizant of our own emotional health.

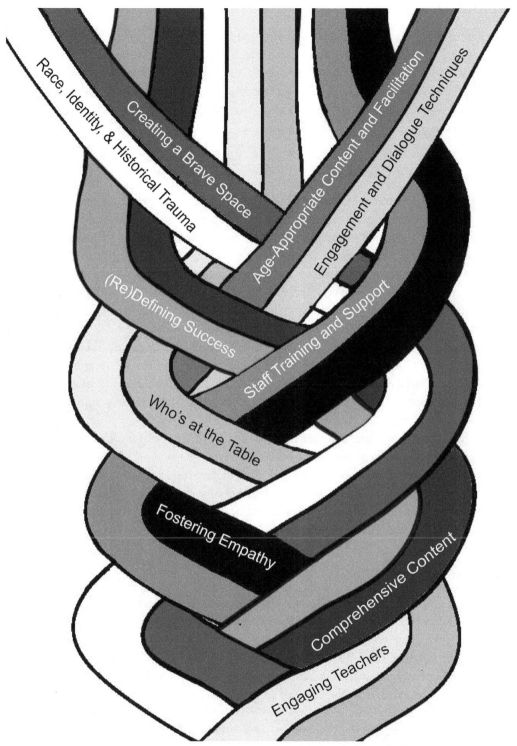

Figure 0.1.   Ten Components to Interpreting Slavery with Children and Teens. Drawing by Yasmine R.R. Robinson

(Re)Defining Success

Developing successful experiences—school tours, field trips, intergenerational programs—about slavery is more than just historical research and some hands-on activities. There is work your institution must do before developing any programs. This includes mission/vision alignment, goal setting, selecting pedagogical techniques, and considering what terminology to use. Success will look different at each organization/site, and sometimes it may mean giving up what you have done for a long time.

Comprehensive Content

A comprehensive portrait of slavery in the United States must include scenes of enslaved people forced to work in great numbers on southern plantations. It should also include the lives of enslaved domestic servants, coachmen, and skilled craftsman. Those enslaved in this country include dockworkers in Boston, New York, and Philadelphia; lone enslaved laborers of households in Connecticut and Massachusetts; and Rhode Island blacksmiths. Enslaved men and women also traveled to the Midwest and the West with their enslavers, where, among other occupations, many toiled alone on small family farms. Comprehensive interpretation covers the great diversity of experiences of slavery and the ways in which those who were enslaved engaged in active resistance against enslavement. The chapter titled "Comprehensive Content and Contested Historical Narratives" in *Interpreting Slavery at Museums and Historic Sites* "explores ways in which our traditional historical narratives make slavery a treacherous topic for interpretation and considers how to help staff and visitors assimilate new information about the history of slavery."[9]

It is important that students understand the history of slavery in the United States starts in Africa, therefore we must put U.S. history in the context of world history. The fact that slavery was an essential ingredient in the founding of the United States is key to the longevity and complexity of the institution and its vestiges of systemic racism and discrimination. The stories and legacies of slavery are broad and deep, and it is incumbent upon all historic sites to share the interconnected narratives.

Who's at the Table

Developing programs on the topic of slavery is a multi-person task and requires the input of not just historians and museum educators, but of child psychologists, teachers, education professors, descendent communities, and even students themselves. When you plot out your development timeline, think about when and how you will involve experts and stakeholders—the earlier and more often the better. *Interpreting Slavery at Museums and Historic Sites* includes a chapter titled "The Necessity of Community Involvement: Talking about Slavery in the 21st Century," by Dina A. Bailey and Richard C. Cooper, that offers strategies for developing and implementing a community involvement plan to ensure a more relevant and successful institution.

Creating a Brave Space

Asking students to confront the challenging history and legacies of slavery can be daunting—for them, their teachers, and museum staff. By establishing a brave, calm, and respectful space, students can take intellectual and emotional risks to discuss the content. A thoughtful, skilled facilitator, along with established rules for dialogue, can help students feel emboldened to share thoughts and experiences, thereby articulating the relevance they find in the historical figures and the legacies of the institution.

Age-Appropriate Content and Facilitation

Young people are not empty slates. They bring knowledge and experience to the discussion, just like adults. With guidance from a facilitator, they can build new understandings and find relevance. Although younger children have a hard time understanding the concept of slavery, there are ways in which they can connect on a human level with those who were enslaved. Being held in bondage is not something a six-year-old, or even a twelve-year-old, will completely understand. But they do understand fairness and kindness, and they can make comparisons to their lives and those of the enslaved. At any age, students need guidance when learning about slavery and researching developmentally appropriate content and techniques is essential. Educators can help students find relevance in and emotional connections with the content. Students need to understand why the people of the past are important to today, and how they are empowered toward agency and action in their own lives.

Fostering Empathy

Emotions are closely entangled with all aspects of history, especially when it comes to matters of identity. Educator Ian Phillips notes, if students "treat people in the past as less than fully human and do not respond to those people's hopes and fears, they have hardly begun to understand what history is about."[10] Therefore, it is critical we use techniques that help students empathize with those who were enslaved. Without a conscious attempt to encourage this empathy, the study of slavery can easily focus attention solely on the perspective of the enslavers who benefited from slavery. We cannot educate students on the mechanisms of slavery and fail to show them the longitudinal impact of the institution on the human beings it affected/affects the most.

Engagement and Dialogue Techniques

Selecting appropriate engagement techniques, including dialogue facilitation and hands-on learning, is key to creating a successful school program. Learning is inherently active and occurs best when our minds *and* bodies are engaged. Physical, emotional, and social engagement are all integral to the learning experience. Go-to program techniques like role-play and simulation can be emotionally harmful for students and can trivialize enslavement and the experiences of enslaved people. It is important to think purposefully and creatively about how to engage students with historic structures, landscapes, objects, and documents. Actively engaging students with historical actors and narratives can help them build deeper understandings and a desire to seek additional information. Building dialogue with effective questioning techniques is essential for helping students engage with the content.

Staff Training and Support

To effectively interpret slavery for any audience, an organization must invest in *all* its staff—from frontline to directors—providing training as well as ongoing emotional and intellectual support. It is essential for public historians and educators to put in significant work before they can expect to work effectively with students on this challenging history. Staff training is not just about historical content, it must also include sessions on facilitation techniques, developing open-ended questions, discussions about race and identity, implicit bias awareness, and much more. Investing time and resources in staff training and ongoing emotional support is what makes for a robust student experience and promotes a healthy work environment. I cannot stress enough the importance of ongoing support of staff, especially for the African American members of your team. It makes a positive difference in your workplace, and in the personal and professional lives of your staff.

Teacher Engagement

Classroom teachers should be part of any successful school program—from the development of a program, to preparing students for the visit and reflecting on it back in the classroom, to engaging in their own learning through professional development. When you include teachers in your process from the beginning to end, they will be more invested in the content, and in your site and its story. Investing time and resources in teachers will help create a better experience for them and their students. Whether the support is intellectual (contextual resources, primary documents, a pre-visit lesson) or emotional (counseling on discussing race/racism in the classroom, a community of practice), teachers and students will benefit.

This framework aims to move the field forward in its collective conversation about the interpretation of slavery with young audiences—acknowledging the shortcomings of the past and acting in the present to develop inclusive interpretation of slavery. When an organization commits to doing school and family programs on the topic of slavery, it makes a promise to past and future generations to keep alive the memory of long-silenced millions and to raise awareness of the racist legacies of slavery in our society today. It is time for the public history field to contribute to a more equitable future for all United States' citizens, and we can do that through our school and youth programs.

> Discrimination and segregation have long permeated much of American life; they now threaten the future of every American. The movement apart can be reversed. . . . It is the realization of common opportunities for all within a single society. . . . From every American it will require new attitudes, new understanding, and, above all, new will.[11]

As we work toward a better present and future for all, our colleague Richard Josey of Collective Journeys asks us to consider one question: "What kind of ancestor will you be?"[12]

Notes

1. Glenn Collins, "A 'Main Event' in Old New York," *New York Times*, September 27, 2005; accessed October 17, 2020, https://www.nytimes.com/2005/09/27/arts/design/a-main-event -in-old-new-york.html.
2. Andre Perry, "Slavery Still Shapes All of Our Lives, Yet Students Aren't Taught Its History," The Hechinger Report, August 20, 2019; accessed January 30, 2021, https://hechingerreport .org/slavery-still-shapes-all-of-our-lives-yet-students-arent-taught-its-history/.
3. This book deals primarily with interpersonal school programs, with only a few references to translating the theory and practice to exhibitions or other written interpretive materials. As you read, you will recognize why I feel that comprehensively and conscientiously facilitated experiences are the best way to interpret the history and legacies of slavery with young people. Hence, my focus is on those interpretive techniques. I encourage you to explore how you can apply the theories and practices cited in the book to your exhibits and other written interpretive materials.
4. Dontavius Williams, Facebook post, October 3, 2020.
5. "9th of July 1640," *Encyclopedia Virginia*, accessed October 10, 2020, https://www.encyclopedia virginia.org/general_court_responds_to_runaway_servants_and_slaves_1640.
6. "Report of the National Advisory Commission on Civil Disorders—Summary of Report," Eisenhower Foundation, accessed October 10, 2020, http://www.eisenhowerfoundation.org/ docs/kerner.pdf.
7. Kristin L. Gallas and James DeWolf Perry, ed. *Interpreting Slavery at Museums and Historic Sites* (Lanham, MD: Rowman and Littlefield, 2015). Contributing authors: Dina Bailey, Tricia Brooks, Richard Cooper, Conny Graft, Linnea Grim, Katherine Kane, Nicole Moore.
8. James DeWolf Perry, an initial collaborator on this project, assisted with the development of this framework.
9. Kristin L. Gallas and James DeWolf Perry, ed. *Interpreting Slavery at Museums and Historic Sites* (Lanham, MD: Rowman and Littlefield, 2015), xvi.
10. Ian Phillips, "Teaching History: Developing as a Reflective Secondary Teacher" (London: Sage Publications, Ltd., 2008), 224.
11. "Report of the National Advisory Commission on Civil Disorders—Summary of Report."
12. Richard Josey, Collective Journeys, accessed December 22, 2018, http://www.collectivejour neys.org.

CHAPTER 1

Race, Identity, and Historical Trauma

"Children have never been very good at listening to their elders, but they have never failed to imitate them."[1] —James Baldwin

S ADULTS, *we* can no longer let our silence on race and slavery be the example for our children to imitate. *We* must not be silent. *We* must tell stories of trauma and stories of agency. *We* must not perpetuate the trauma of slavery by hiding it from young people. *We* must confront the modern legacies of race that rest on the foundation of slavery and engage students in responsible and respectful conversations. *We* must call out and educate family, friends, and colleagues when they make a not-so-subtle, veiled racist joke or prejudiced assumption. *We* must do the work.

To my fellow white people, *you* are going to have to deal with the "icky" feelings that arise when someone brings up race. *You* must listen with an open and empathetic mind when your Black colleagues tell you what it is like to be the subject of overt and implicit racism. *You* must take it seriously when a Black colleague calls you out for an expression of white privilege. *You* must confront and examine your own implicit biases. And, yes, *you* are going to have to make the space to talk with your student visitors about the subjection of Black people in the institution of slavery, the ensuing 150+ years of socially and politically accepted discrimination, and the modern-day effects of more than four hundred years of oppression of the African American community.

We Might Not Want Race to Matter, But It Does.

Our brains are wired to notice differences in other humans; this is part of our fight-or-flight instincts. What matters most is how we understand and act on those differences.[2] Multiple research studies have shown that children learn, both explicitly and implicitly, from the adults in their lives.[3] Children as young as four notice, and can articulate, differences in the way people look.[4] "White children as young as six are aware of their racial identity," Akilah

Dulin-Keita et al., writes. "[And] preschool children use racist language to produce harmful results, to evoke emotional reactions by victims, and to recreate social hierarchies."[5] Even though race is a critical component to everyone's life, adults often note they are "color blind" and are raising their children to be so as well. This is disheartening on several levels. First, a person's race is integral to their identity and ignoring someone's race is denying part of their humanity. Secondly, we live in a racialized society. A society in which

> interracial marriage rates are low, residential separation and socioeconomic inequality are the norm, our definitions of personal identity and our choices of intimate associations reveal racial distinctiveness, and where we are never unaware of the race of a person with whom we interact. . . . [A] society that allocates differential economic, political, social, and even psychological rewards to groups along racial lines; lines that are socially constructed. . . . A society wherein race matters profoundly for differences in life experiences, life opportunities, and social relationships.[6]

Talking about race and the history of slavery is challenging, especially when you are talking with young people or someone not well versed in the subject. Our first instinct is often to ignore the subject altogether, but by disregarding it, we perpetuate a cycle in which young people learn to hide their feelings on the subject. Having the discussion stirs up emotions in everyone—Black and white. Our identities—specifically our race—play a role in how we tell the story of slavery and how we receive it. This chapter examines the ways race and identity impact our work, audience reception of the story, and the trauma the stories can inflict on both staff and student visitors.

Race and Identity

Race: A way to categorize and divide human beings. It is a social construct, not biological, and relates to the grouping of people based on skin color and other physical characteristics. It is often used for creating and emphasizing the dominance of one group over another.[7]

Identity: The "set of visible and invisible characteristics we use to categorize and define ourselves and those around us (e.g., gender, race, age, religion, etc.). Identity shapes our experience by influencing the ways we see ourselves and the ways others see us."[8]

The discussion of slavery is inextricably linked to the ideas of race and identity, and we must address the two in tandem, however challenging it might be. Dr. Howard Dodson, chief of the New York Public Library's Schomburg Center for Research in Black Culture, notes how the subject of slavery heightens emotions. "With Blacks [slavery] has been a subject of embarrassment. I know that was true with me when I was growing up. And with whites, it's fear of being charged with being guilty because of the sins of the fathers."[9] By examining and acknowledging our identities and those of our student visitors, we can more openly and respectfully address the subject of race and slavery.

Identity of the Interpreter/Educator

Just as any discussion of slavery must include ideas of race and identity, these concepts also play a major role in how we prepare and deliver education programs. People hold multiple individual and collective identities simultaneously. For example, someone might be a daughter (individual identity) and call herself an American (collective). Sometimes our identities are based on mythology and romanticism, like being the great-great grandson of a "kind" slaveowner (individual identity) and subscribing to its Lost Cause mythology (collective). No matter how we identify—race or otherwise—it is important for us to examine who we are, what biases we might hold, and how those affect our ability to talk with and listen to our student visitors.

Thankfully, there are many excellent tools available to help us work through our concerns. Books such as *White Fragility: Why It's So Hard for White People to Talk about Racism* (Robin DiAngelo, 2018), *So You Want to Talk about Race* (Ijeoma Oluo, 2018), and *How to Be an Antiracist* (Ibram X. Kendi, 2019) are great places to start. The Southern Poverty Law Center's Learning for Justice curriculum, the American Anthropological Association's *Understanding Race* project, or teacher resources from Facing History and Ourselves provide step-by-step lesson plans that can help you and your staff confront these matters. There are even resources specific to the museum field, including *Museums and Race* and *MASS Action (Museums as Sites for Social Action)*.[10]

We must also recognize that even our youngest visitors may question the knowledge and skills of the interpreter based on his or her race. Black students may perceive an older white person as lacking emotional sensitivity to deliver a comprehensive story of slavery and might assume more truth and solidarity from a Black interpreter. White students may anticipate hearing the "good master" narrative from a white interpreter and feel betrayed when they receive a narrative that crushes that myth. White students may also distrust African American staff members, anticipating a story biased toward the enslaved. Upending long-held narratives can be challenging. It helps if we explicitly acknowledge how identity plays a role in historical narratives, as it should help students adjust their expectations and open their minds to learning.

Identity of the Visitor

While children as young as four can identify that people have different skin colors (i.e., race) they have not yet internalized the societal "norms" that accompany this fact.[11] From a very young age, youth are bombarded with societal messages of white privilege and begin to discern the implicit and explicit meaning of one's skin color. Beverly Daniel Tatum reports that students of color, particularly Black and Latinx students "are socialized to develop an identity that integrates competencies for transacting race, ethnicity, and culture in everyday life."[12] They learn from their family, school, the media, friends, and politicians that everything in life is a lesson on how to operate and survive in our society as a member of the non-dominant culture. These teachings follow them to our museums and historic sites, and they cross our thresholds with a wealth of knowledge and experience on what it means to engage in verbal and non-verbal interactions about race and racism.

I often hear stories from museum educators and interpreters who say that they adjust their interpretation based on the race of the students in their groups. This confuses me because I believe we should be delivering the same comprehensive content and emotionally conscientious material to all student visitors. White staff members tell me they get anxious when they have a group of Black students, because the staff members are afraid of saying the wrong thing and being called racist. While it is valid to consider different emotional states in anticipation of a new audience, the most important thing to remember is that if you have done the work to better understand the dynamics at play for visitors, you should be equipped with the tools to engage students in a conversation about slavery and race. (See chapter 8 for staff training.) Remember, if you make students the center of the interpretation—asking them to express their feelings and points of relevance—you take the focus off yourself (where it should not be anyway) and put it on the content and your students' relationship to the content. By establishing a brave space and engaging students in dialogue, we can help them make connections between their identities and the historical content. (See chapter 3 for establishing a brave space and chapter 7 for dialogue techniques.

Learning and Trauma

Trauma: "An experience of severe psychological distress following any terrible or life-threatening event."[13]

Historical Trauma: "Begins with the subjugation of a minority population by a dominant majority group. Subjugation is maintained through violence, hateful mythology, and the creation of social and political inequalities that evolve into a totalitarian system of racism and discrimination. Its applications in contemporary society continue to marginalize the target population."[14]

Intergenerational Trauma: "A traumatic event that began years prior to the current generation and has impacted the ways in which individuals within a family understand, cope with, and heal from trauma."[15]

Post-Traumatic Stress Disorder: "A mental health condition that develops in response to experiencing or witnessing an extremely stressful event involving the threat of death or extreme bodily harm. . . . The condition may manifest in anxiety-like symptoms, emotional numbness or dysphoria, anger and aggression."[16]

Post-Traumatic Slave Syndrome: A theory that explains the cause of adaptive survival behaviors in African American communities, as a result of multigenerational oppression from centuries of chattel slavery, followed by the subjugation of systemic racism and the absence of opportunity to heal or access to benefits in the society.[17]

Our Collective Trauma

The history of the United States is one of trauma and violence. The trauma of the Revolutionary War violently ripped the colonies from England. Along the way the colonists and new Americans decimated the lives of millions of indigenous people. The myth of American

Exceptionalism, "that America's values, political system, and history are unique and worthy of universal admiration," is based on the traumatic reality of enslavement, murder, rape, and stolen land.[18] When we tell our history in classrooms and public forums, the stories of war have long predominated. Political assassinations, First Amendment protests, laws restricting civil rights—all these episodes are traumatic to someone. Society is quick to recognize the trauma beset on individuals—a rape, sudden death, or injury—but what about realizing that trauma can have long-lasting collective effects on a community? We need to recognize trauma is both individual and collective.

The traumatic history of slavery sits on the surface of every aspect of life—for Black *and* white people—in the United States, yet much to our detriment, we fail to recognize it. As Timothy P. Brown writes in "Trauma, Museums and the Future of Pedagogy,"

> America still suffers from the legacy of slavery and systematic oppression of black people and genocide of first nations; it also suffers from the residual effects of global, imperialistic endeavours, as evident in the terrorist attacks on the United States. In this context, trauma is not just a condition that is specific to certain groups; trauma characterises life in the twentieth and twenty-first centuries. Indeed, the effects of trauma can reverberate through a community to such a degree that the very notion of a national and cultural identity is kept in a perpetual state of crisis.[19]

As an integral part of our history, slavery is part of our collective memory and sharing the collective narrative instead of ignoring it can help us all recover from the trauma. This trauma demands social recognition and needs to be understood as the root of intergenerational trauma, the post-traumatic slave syndrome theory, in the African American community.[20] This simple act of acknowledgement can begin to relieve the burden on those who have been traumatized. Acknowledging those collective memories allows us to share stories, bear witness, and heal together. Brown also notes,

> one can speak of traumatized communities as something distinct from traumatized persons. Sometimes the tissues of community can be damaged in much the same way as the tissues of mind and body . . . but even when that does not happen, traumatic wounds inflicted on individuals can combine to create a mood, ethos—a group culture, almost— that is different from (and more than) the sum of the private wounds that make it up.[21]

Museums and historic sites can play an integral role in helping individuals and communities recognize and heal from the collective trauma of slavery and racism, and the lasting damage done to the African American community. School programs help by telling the whole story, navigating away from the mythological happy slave / good master narrative, and stressing the importance of understanding that the success and wealth of the white slaveholding family was solely reliant on the forced labor of those they enslaved. This acknowledgement is key to helping young people understand the root of this racist trauma in our country.

Establishing a healing or restorative truth of slavery can be a highly contested process, as most people hew closely to their personal truths.[22] In their communities, states, and regions, museums can help by providing the factual/forensic truths about slavery and its legacies. This process will generate strong emotions, as we are addressing historical events and people that caused serious harm to generations of African Americans. Throughout this process, we must work to minimize the trauma by speaking the truth and implementing strategies that care for students' (and our) social-emotional health. We need to stop covering up the pain and damage of slavery with lies of happy slaves and face the white supremacist foundation on which the country was built. While it may not result in changing the state of systemic institutional racism, it will help address the implicit biases, overt racism, and internalized oppression our student visitors embody.

Trauma in African American Children

Imagine living every day of your life in fear. Imagine having to remember a set of rules designed just for people like you:

- Keep your hands where police officers can see them.
- Do not talk back.
- Do not be lazy.
- Avoid being alone with a white woman you do not know.
- Do not wear a hoodie.
- Do not hang out on street corners after dark.
- Be wary of the police.
- Do not be overly emotional.

These are just a sampling of rules for survival in a white-dominant society that Black families communicate to their children. Some are learned through direct communication, others indirectly. These survival "rules" have been thrust upon the Black community by a white supremacist culture. Frustrations and anger about these unwritten rules of being Black in America are part of their upbringing. They are survival mechanisms developed over generations, from 1619 to today. As Timothy P. Brown puts it, "Trauma for African-Americans has involved not only the difficulty in confronting the Middle Passage but also the persistence of racism in America."[23] The intergenerational nature of the trauma extends to their enslaved ancestors who repeatedly suffered physical, psychological, and emotional abuse. The resulting mental health issues (PTSD, depression, substance abuse, anxiety, anger, and chronic grief) are prevalent in their descendants (a similar pattern is found in the descendants of Holocaust survivors).[24] The need for these survival strategies further illustrates the inequities and deficits in the United States. Black citizens should not have to bear daily microaggressions, the fear of "driving while Black," being told they are a "credit to their race," or repressing feelings to avoid being labeled as the "angry Black woman," in a land where all men are purportedly created equal.

Students who identify or present as African American come to us with knowledge about what it means to be Black in the United States. The world around them—popular culture, historical myths, mainstream media, economic disparities, and even politicians—provides young people with cues that suggest they are somehow "less than" white people.

This constant barrage of negative messages can lead to an internalized racism, a defining characteristic of Post-Traumatic Slave Syndrome, which is identified as the following:

1. A "systemic oppression in reaction to racism that has a life of its own. In other words, just as there is a system in place that reinforces the power and expands the privilege of white people, there is a system in place that actively discourages and undermines the power of people and communities of color and mires us in our own oppressions."[25]
2. Because the cause is systemic and structural, it cannot be viewed as self-hatred or low self-esteem. It must "be understood as a system to be grappled with by people and communities of color in the same way that even the most committed anti-racist white people must continue to grapple personally and in community with their own and other white people's privilege."[26]
3. "Internalized racism negatively impacts people of color intra-culturally and cross-culturally. Because race is a social and political construct that comes out of particular histories of domination and exploitation between Peoples, people of colors' internalized racism often leads to great conflict among and between them as other concepts of power—such as ethnicity, culture, nationality and class—are collapsed in misunderstanding. Especially when race is confused with nationality and ethnicity, internalized racism often manifests in different cultural and ethnic groups being pitted against each other for the scarce resources that racism leaves for people who do not have white privilege. This can create a hierarchy based on closeness to the white norm."[27]

We must recognize that internalized racism is something some students may grapple with, and we must anticipate that learning about the traumatic realities of slavery might cause an emotional reaction. This content is inherently emotional, and it might blindside a student who is not ready for it.

Recommendations for conscientiously addressing race and trauma:

- [Establish] a sense of psychological safety and trust so that students can express their perspectives and listen respectfully to others' perspectives, even when there are disagreements.
- Prior to engaging in the discussion, set up options and provide clear directions for managing overwhelming emotional responses related to the discussion [e.g., stepping out of the tour for a moment to debrief with a teacher or friend].
- Honor and respect differences in emotions and responses just as you do differences in perspectives.
- Validate and honor students' experiences and emotions rather than trying to convince them that they no longer have a rational reason to feel that way. Avoid telling them that their past experiences should not affect their current beliefs.

- Validate and de-escalate emotions when possible, but also realize that some students, especially those who have experienced complex trauma, often have difficulty identifying, expressing, and managing emotions.
- Check in with students periodically throughout the discussion, to ensure that they are managing emotional experiences in a healthy manner and that they continue to feel safe.
- Be authentic and respectful with students. It is natural to worry whether you are saying "the right thing." However, respectful authenticity is often more important because the chief contributor to a psychologically safe classroom is learning to have honest, albeit hard, conversations in healthy and constructive ways.
- Use processes (such as restorative or dialogue circles) to facilitate and support authentic discussions, even when conflict may be at the core.
- [Build into your program] a variety of ways for students to deal with their emotions in productive, constructive, and meaningful ways. Consider devoting time to physical activities, art, music, and/or quiet time following these discussions.
- Remember that no one has control over the impact their words have on others. Avoid responding angrily or defensively if someone interprets your—or someone else's—words differently than they were intended. As best as possible, attempt to clarify.
- Help students understand the connection between historical trauma, systemic racism, and community trauma in communities of color.
- Understand the culture in which you are working and find cultural references that will resonate with your students.
- Give students opportunities to share cultural stories and experiences in a variety of ways, such as using art and music, to validate their worldviews and give them an opportunity to develop their own interventions for coping and healing.
- Offer empathy and understanding to students who express distrust and distress, as these emotions are key to acknowledging the past hurt.
- Use local and/or national issues to highlight the pervasive harms of racism on individuals and on communities.
- [Share stories of] various movements in racial and social justice history to illustrate how individuals can make a difference.
- Help students think broadly about their options and opportunities for leadership. Some options might include organizing dialogues, small gatherings, or school events to discuss race and trauma, and to advocate for equity and inclusion; volunteering with local grassroots organizations; or helping to make messages of equity and inclusivity visible on school grounds, such as designing and displaying posters.[28]

We must be aware of and prepared for how students might receive a comprehensive narrative of slavery. Brandon Dillard, manager of historic interpretation at Thomas Jefferson's Monticello, shared his thoughts about training staff to facilitate these types of discussions with young visitors.

Telling the story of slavery as anything less than monstrously wrong fails to convey the truth. But we can't be too direct or blunt with children, because again, most of them lack the tools to process that kind of information and may well be grappling with their own traumatic pasts. Some of them may be triggered to re-experience the trauma of their own lives, and . . . they don't have the tools to process that re-triggering. . . . So, an older rich white woman talking about racism to a group of black third-graders involves an awful lot of careful consideration and negotiation on [the staff's] part.

You can find more information about training staff on race and identity awareness in chapter 8.

Most of the time our school groups come to us as a big question mark. Even with multi-visit experiences (either in school, on-site, or virtual), we rarely even garner the most basic insight into their backgrounds. Therefore, we must be confident and competent in our abilities to address stories of historical trauma and the emotions they might stir in our student visitors. Students do not always possess the tools to process the traumatic history or their emotions, which makes comprehensive staff training and the development of empathetic and pedagogically sound activities that much more important.

Figure 1.1. A group of students during a school program at Thomas Jefferson's Monticello. ©Thomas Jefferson Foundation at Monticello

Notes

1. John Schwab, "James Baldwin Quotes on Race, America, and Identity," June 1, 2020; accessed July 31, 2020, https://www.inspiringalley.com/james-baldwin-quotes/.
2. Leslie Henderson, "Why Our Brains See the World as 'Us' versus 'Them,'" *The Conversation*, November 12, 2014; accessed August 25, 2020, https://theconversation.com/why-our-brains-see-the-world-as-us-versus-them-98661.
3. Akilah Dulin-Keita et al., "The Defining Moment: Children's Conceptualization of Race and Experiences with Racial Discrimination," *Ethnic and Racial Studies* 34, no. 4 (April 2011); accessed August 25, 2020, https://www.ncbi.nlm.nih.gov/pmc/articles/PMC3083924/.
4. Debbie Sonu, "Playing Slavery in First Grade: When 'Developmental Appropriateness' Goes Awry in the Progressive Classroom," *Multicultural Perspectives* 22, no. 2 (May 2020): 111.
5. Dulin-Keita et al., "The Defining Moment."
6. Michael Emerson and Christian Smith, *Divided by Faith* (New York: Oxford University Press, 2000), 7.
7. "Looking at Race and Racial Identity in Children's Books," Learning for Justice, Southern Poverty Law Center, accessed July 31, 2020, https://www.tolerance.org/classroom-resources/tolerance-lessons/looking-at-race-and-racial-identity-in-childrens-books.
8. "Let's Talk! Facilitating Critical Conversations with Students," *Teaching Tolerance*, Southern Poverty Law Center, accessed July 31, 2020, https://www.tolerance.org/magazine/publications/lets-talk.
9. Glenn Collins, "A 'Main Event' in Old New York," *New York Times*, September 27, 2005; accessed July 31, 2020, https://www.nytimes.com/2005/09/27/arts/design/a-main-event-in-old-new-york.html.
10. Museums and Race: https://museumsandrace.org/. MASS Action: https://www.museumaction.org/.
11. Sonu, "Playing Slavery in First Grade," 111.
12. Beverly Daniel Tatum, *Why Are All the Black Kids Sitting Together in the Cafeteria: And Other Conversations about Race* (New York: Basic Books, 2017), 134.
13. "What Is Trauma," *Psychology Today*, accessed August 7, 2020, https://www.psychologytoday.com/us/basics/trauma.
14. Graham Danzera et al., "White Psychologists and African Americans' Historical Trauma: Implications for Practice," *Journal of Aggression, Maltreatment & Trauma* 25, no. 4 (2016): 354.
15. Támara Hill, "Should Mental Health Professionals Understand Intergenerational Trauma?," The Association for Child and Adolescent Mental Health, December 18, 2017; accessed August 7, 2020, https://www.acamh.org/blog/intergenerational-trauma/#:~:text=I%20tend%20to%20define%20inter,with%2C%20and%20heal%20from%20trauma.
16. "What Is Post-Traumatic Stress Disorder," *Psychology Today*, accessed August 7, 2020, https://www.psychologytoday.com/intl/basics/post-traumatic-stress-disorder.
17. Joy Degruy, "Post-Traumatic Slave Syndrome," accessed August 28, 2020, https://www.joydegruy.com/post-traumatic-slave-syndrome.
18. Stephen M. Walt, "The Myth of American Exceptionalism," October 11, 2011; accessed August 22, 2020, https://foreignpolicy.com/2011/10/11/the-myth-of-american-exceptionalism/.
19. Timothy P. Brown, "Trauma, Museums and the Future of Pedagogy," *Third Text* 18, no.4 (2004), 247.

20. Historian and author Ibram X. Kendi counters DeGruy's theory, saying, "I am hoping that the believers in PTSS realize that their theory is premised on racist notions of degenerate Black people. I am hoping that the believers in PTSS realize that any idea that suggests any group of Black people are inferior in any way is a racist idea. . . . Like every other popular racist theory, post-traumatic slave syndrome seems so logical. No one can credibly deny that generations of Black people have suffered trauma from the whips of racist America. . . . No one can credibly deny that there are individual Blacks who behave negatively in all sorts of ways, sometimes as a result of trauma. No one can credibly deny that Black people deserve reparations for stolen lives and labor. But the logic and progressive flair of PTSS does not make it true. PTSS theorists rely on anecdotal evidence. And in customary racist fashion, they generalize the anecdotal negativities of *individual* Blacks in order to establish the problem of negative *Black* behaviors. PTSS theorists have not proven these negative behaviors are a Black problem; that Black people behave more negatively than other groups, let alone that these negative Black behaviors largely stem from a heritage of trauma." Ibram X. Kendi, "Post-Traumatic Slave Syndrome Is a Racist Idea," *Black Perspectives*, June 21, 2016, https://www.aaihs.org/post-traumatic-slave-syndrome-is-a-racist-idea/.
21. Brown, "Trauma, Museums and the Future of Pedagogy," 249.
22. Donald W. Shriver, Jr., "Truths for Reconciliation: An American Perspective," National Park Service Common Learning Portal, updated April 4, 2017; accessed February 2, 2021, https://mylearning.nps.gov/library-resources/truths-for-reconciliation-an-american-perspective/.
23. Brown, "Trauma, Museums and the Future of Pedagogy," 255.
24. Graham Danzera et al., "White Psychologists and African Americans' Historical Trauma: Implications for Practice, *Journal of Aggression, Maltreatment & Trauma* 25, no 4 (2016): 354.
25. Donna K. Bivens, "What Is Internalized Racism," page 44, accessed August 14, 2020, https://www.racialequitytools.org/resourcefiles/What_is_Internalized_Racism.pdf.
26. Bivens, "What Is Internalized Racism," 44.
27. Bivens, "What Is Internalized Racism," 44.
28. Excerpted from "Addressing Race and Trauma in the Classroom," The National Child Traumatic Stress Network, n.d.; accessed January 29, 2021, https://www.nctsn.org/sites/default/files/resources/addressing_race_and_trauma_in_the_classroom_educators.pdf.

CHAPTER 2

(Re)Defining a Successful Experience

"There are no set ways to interpret challenging histories. The work of providing museum learning around a contested history must be a constant negotiation between the subject, the resources, and the audience."[1] —Samantha Cairns

DEVELOPING EXPERIENCES—school programs, field trips, family tours—about slavery entails more than historical research and hands-on activities. Your institution must undertake some foundational work to define a "successful" experience before you can develop one. This work includes aligning mission and vision to the project, setting goals, selecting appropriate educational pedagogy, and considering what terminology to use. These basic building blocks will set you up for success in the work to come.

Aligning Institutional Mission, Vision, and Values

Before developing any programs or exhibits about slavery, ensure your institution has a solid foundation on which to build. Your "on-the-ground" intentions for telling these stories might lead to some institutional changes that will affect the organization's basic identity (mission, vision, and values) and the people who shape it (the board and staff). The mission states your purpose; the vision scopes the future; and values ground your beliefs.[2] How do your mission and vision statements reflect your institution's purpose of telling a more comprehensive, conscientious story of slavery? Is the entire board and staff on the same page about the journey that you are on? Are your stakeholders? Redefining mission, vision, and values should be an internal (board, staff, volunteers) and external process. Include a diverse group of stakeholders, comprising members of descendent communities, educators, historians, faith groups, and others, in the process. Doing so early, and with intention, helps these stakeholders be more invested in your site and story.

Start with the mission statement, which the American Alliance of Museums says should state "why the museum exists and who benefits as a result of its efforts."[3] If slavery's story is integral to your site, or a major topic in your museum, explicitly mention it in your mission statement. For example, the Montpelier Foundation, which operates James Madison's historic home, positions itself as "A memorial to James Madison and the Enslaved Community, a museum of American history, and a center for constitutional education that engages the public with the enduring legacy of Madison's most powerful idea: government by the people."[4] The mission explicitly states whom the site strives to remember. Notice that the foundation has even gone as far as to capitalize "Enslaved Community" as a proper noun, giving them as much prominence as Madison.

Royall House and Slave Quarters in Medford, Massachusetts, is an excellent example of a reframed mission statement that reflects a more holistic history of the house. In 2005 the board of the Royall House Association changed the way it thought about the property, the historic structures, and the people who once lived and worked there. The revamped mission states that the organization "explores the meanings of freedom and independence before, during, and since the American Revolution, in the context of a household of wealthy Loyalists and enslaved Africans."[5] This new mission is inclusive of a wider variety of historical stories and of how the site's history connects to issues of freedom and independence today.[6] Their new mission statement also changed the focus of their school programs, which now center solely on the enslaved experience.

The board and staff of President Lincoln's Cottage, the residence where Lincoln wrote the Emancipation Proclamation, chose "a home for brave ideas" as their guiding vision. The statement affirms a commitment to foster difficult discussions of issues surrounding slavery and its legacies. The board and staff acknowledge the "power of place" and how stories of leadership in the face of adversity are relevant today. "We witness that the stories of what happened here historically have the power to bring out the leader in any person today, inspiring courageous ideas, respectful dialogue, and thoughtful compromise."[7] Programs focus on empowering young people and helping them develop principled leadership skills, encouraging them to take lessons from the past and apply them today.

Once you have established a mission and vision, I recommend that museums and historic sites articulate a values statement specifically for interpreting the history of slavery. This statement defines the beliefs and culture of the organization, and will inform how you want to research, reflect on, and interpret the institution of slavery, and those whose lives it affected (in the past and present). When setting values, think about what your organization believes in and how you want to apply that to researching and telling your site's slavery-related stories.

When asked how they wanted to treat the history, people of the past, their colleagues, and stakeholders, the leadership team of Morven Museum and Gardens—home to Richard Stockton, a signer of the Declaration of Independence, and those he enslaved, as well as five New Jersey governors—said they wanted to treat the history as if it were a person. They decided on the two-word phrase "respectful and reflective," which signified their desire to be respectful of the history, do accurate and thorough research, and be inclusive of a variety of voices, past and present. They also strove to be reflective, offering themselves and visitors a chance to be thoughtful about the history and its legacies. This statement helped them focus as they embarked on the development of their new permanent exhibit, *Historic Morven: A Window into America's Past*. The exhibition presents the story of the house's owners, "while adding the voices of the many people who lived and worked at Morven, including women, children, generations of enslaved men and women, immigrant servants, and later, employees."[8]

Your values statement will be a touchstone for your work, a beacon that will guide you when you feel lost. Archivist Dr. Susan Nalezyty of Georgetown Visitation Preparatory School in Washington, DC, the historic home of an order of Catholic nuns and those they enslaved, said about their values statement, "During tense moments with how to proceed, . . . [the values] guide us in our decisions . . . honesty, humanity, and humility. . . . It is impressive the power of sorting out that values statement, because it's a good measure of our efforts, comforting sometimes."[9] As it has for the staff and sisters at Visitation, the values statement serves a public-facing declaration that clearly presents your institution's sentiments and intentions to stakeholders and visitors.

As you engage in this foundational work, it is important to consider how your new direction and holistic narrative might lead to negative feedback from visitors. While this is unlikely to come from students, it may come from teachers and parent chaperones who are having difficulty comprehending your purpose and/or are uncomfortable with the topic altogether. Do not dismiss them out of hand; strive to engage them in a learning opportunity and help them understand your mission, vision, and values. Those foundational statements are there to support and justify your work. Whether or not the visitor agrees with what you are doing, they have taken notice and you have planted a seed for future learning opportunities.

What Is a Successful Experience?

Every organization/museum must define a successful experience for itself, as success will manifest uniquely for every organization and every audience. To many museum educators, an important marker of a successful youth-centered program—field trip, scout program, out-of-school time, or family program—is whether the youth have fun. We must step back and assess whether "fun" is what makes interpretation successful when the subject of the program is slavery.

Some may argue that interpretation needs to be fun to keep students' attention. In grappling with this, museum educators must rethink the program development process and help teacher and student audiences shift their field trip expectations. "If students are not supposed to have 'fun,'" you may wonder, "how do historic sites and museums know if they have developed a successful program? What are the qualities of successful interpretation with youth, especially with a topic like slavery? Does engagement equal fun?" This chapter offers some interpretive pedagogy you might want to consider when defining and developing a successful program on slavery.

Putting the Learner at the Center

In the formal education world, today's pedagogical researchers are promoting the concept of learner-centered teaching. By putting students in control of their learning, not only are they building content, but they are also developing and practicing communication skills and critical thinking. Learning only happens when the brain is actively engaged, so we must create educational experiences that engage the whole learner: mind, body, and emotions. As veteran Colonial Williamsburg Foundation interpreter James Ingram Jr. notes, "If I have a group that includes children, I always make them a part of what I'm doing. I make them realize how important they are."[10] Ingram is espousing his personal theory of interpretation, but he's also offering us a glimpse of good interpretive practices—learner-centered and inclusive.

While putting the learner at the center of the interpretation, we must consider how the program supports students' skills development, as well as knowledge acquisition. Designing successful experiences should not be about cramming as much content as possible into the tour or program. We should also support the development of historical thinking skills. Programs should support skills such as close-looking, inquiry, deduction, and evaluation, allowing "students to have ownership and responsibility for their learning rather than simply gathering information."[11] These techniques help students make sense of the content by exercising important historical thinking skills, such as contextualization, analysis, and considering multiple perspectives.

For example, the Tsongas Industrial History Center creates learner-centered programs using seven principles the staff developed to define successful experiential learning. The center, an education partnership between the University of Massachusetts Lowell College of Education and Lowell National Historical Park, develops and implements school programs for the park, including programs on the topic of slave-raised cotton that the city's mill turned into textiles. The center's mission is to engage students in experiential learning about the Industrial Revolution and its legacies. The center's staff defines learn-centered experiential learning as:

- *Active*: Learners engage through hand-on activities and simulations.
- *Minds-on*: Learners connect intellectually with content and build deeper understandings.
- *Sensory*: Learners immerse themselves in the historic resources and natural environment.
- *Fun*: Learners have the freedom to play and be creative.
- *Collaborative*: Learners unite through dialogue, by working together, and sharing authority.
- *Inspirational*: Learners feel empowered toward action thinking, agency, and stewardship.
- *Affective*: Learners reflect and make emotional connections.

This framework informs the staff on how to design learner-centered programs. For example, in the program that addresses the cotton-textile manufacturing process (Bale to Bolt), when we talk about the enslaved people who picked the cotton that fed the mills we focus on the minds-on and affective aspects of experiential learning. The center places emphasis on how students are "experiencing" their learning—that is, what are they doing and how is the staff setting them up to be successful in doing so. That provides reasonable ways for the staff to measure outcomes, because they are process outcomes, and to assess the success of the programs and staff.

Design for Experience Instead of Outputs

When shifting to learner-centered learning, think about the behaviors you want students to exhibit during the program: what student behaviors demonstrate they are engaged in learning. Remember that the goal of education should not solely be the acquisition of knowledge, but also of "developing and deepening student understandings" through the learning experience.[12] Therefore, design learning objectives to account for the change in cognitive, practical, and emotional knowledge that students demonstrate during the experience, rather than solely for demonstrable outcomes at the *end* of the program.

During the spring of 2017, I observed a program for a racially diverse group of high school students at Mount Vernon that would have benefited from learner-centered, experiential outcomes. The program script outlined eight objectives in three categories (learning, emotional, and inspirational) that all stated what they want students to "understand" at the end of the program. Because objectives are more than just knowledge to be understood, the institution would have been wiser to devise ways to invite the students to deepen and demonstrate their understanding.

At the end of each "stop" on the tour, the guide posed a rhetorical question or shared an impactful piece of information like, "punishments varied from additional work to being sold away. The worst punishment was being sold to the West Indies, where the work was harder and life expectancy shorter. George Washington only did this three times."[13] There is a lot of information packed into those three short sentences, almost too much, and all of is potentially traumatizing.

After describing the enslaved person's actions that led to the punishment she described, the guide did not unpack these statements or ask the students what they thought. Instead, she shepherded them on to the next stop on the tour. When leaving the stop where this statement was posed, I overheard one student say he thought they were moving too quickly and that he wanted to spend more time at each space. His friends agreed. The fact that students wanted to spend more time at a certain spot on the tour spoke volumes to me. The students wanted to process and discuss the information and questions the guide posed. If the education staff wrote the tour, and gave the tour guide the latitude, to encourage critical thinking and allow students the intellectual space to process their understanding, staff may have been able to see the proof of some of their "understanding" objectives.

During my post–field trip conversation with the site's education staff, the tour guide said she chose to say something pithy and then leave each place abruptly so that the students would have time to think about what she said as they walked. She wanted to give them time to reflect introspectively, to leave them questioning. While this is well intentioned, it is not enough. Yes, it is important to give students "wait time" after you pose a question or provocative statement, but you should follow this with time for students to interact with each other, and to help them process and make connections to find relevance. While not all students will verbalize their thoughts, hearing others share plays an important role in deepening understanding. Students need time to process and discuss this content, especially when it comes to reframing George Washington and his actions as an enslaver. The "drop an interpretive 'bomb'" technique sensationalizes the content, serves to avoid discussing the content, and does not allow for the students to think critically about the topic.

It is hard to measure understanding, especially during a tour of a historic site that does not have an open-ended essay question at the end. To hope that students will understand something by talking at them for an hour does not allow for the full potential of students' emotional and intellectual intelligence. Engaging in dialogue with students, where questions and responses flow from guide to students, students to guide, and students to students, is key to helping students integrate and process the content and their feelings about it. (See chapter 7 on dialogue techniques.) It is important to develop programs that give students a chance to exercise their understanding and that staff are trained in the skills to make that happen. (See chapter 8 for information on staff training.)

The Self-Guided Experience

To accommodate bigger school groups, many larger historic sites use a self-guided visit model. The study of slavery demands we consider whether students will have a successful learning experience with teachers and volunteer chaperones facilitating the visit. Students have a more meaningful learning experience, Alan S. Marcus and associates write, when they "are actively involved with group work and other participatory activities. . . . [The visits] are more effective when there is a specific purpose, when there is an explicit connection to the classroom curriculum, and when the teacher is involved."[14] Can you count on chaperones to engage students in a comprehensive, pedagogically sound, and emotionally safe discussion about slavery? While self-guided visits are efficient for volume, they are not the most successful way for students to access content, particularly the history of slavery. While it may be possible to build an adequate self-guided experience, it can be scary to leave teachers and chaperones in charge of the facilitation, as they may perpetuate mythologies and falsehoods about slavery. They may not have skills to lead pedagogically sound discussions; however, depending on their connections with and knowledge of the students, they may be able to create an emotionally safe environment for sharing. While I do not recommend this model, if you do choose a self-guided experience, think hard about how the experience creates a learner-centered experience and how it provides students with effective and affective connections to the history and legacies of slavery.

Who's at the Table?

If you are building school and youth programs, your first call might be to someone who knows the intellectual and emotional capabilities of children and teens: a child development specialist, professor of education, or child psychologist. Their expertise can provide essential feedback on what is appropriate for kids at a specific age. They can also help address concerns about talking with kids about traumatic topics and how to diffuse situations that may arise with students who are uncomfortable with or distressed by the history and its legacies.

Including classroom teachers in the development process is also helpful, as they will be able to provide feedback on what techniques will work with their students. (See chapter 9 for more on working with teachers.) School programs should line up with state and national curriculum standards for a specific grade level, and teachers will be well versed in those. Teachers can also provide access to students—an instant focus group for prototyping the new program.

Do not forget students—they will know best what works for them. Develop kids' programs *with* them rather than *for* them! Richard Josey encourages us to "work with a classroom of diverse students to build a program they can 'own.' Think of the magic of that!"[15] Before you finalize anything, prototype the program with students and teachers. That way you know what works and what does not work, as well as where you need to provide additional training for your staff.

Choosing the Right Language

When communicating complex concepts to children and teens it is vital to think about what topics and language are age appropriate and what they have already been exposed to. You must introduce your word choice(s) and explain them. For instance, an institution might decide to use the terms "enslaver" and "enslaved" instead of "master" and "slave" because the words more appropriately define people by their actions, or actions put to them, instead of reducing people to nouns. It might be helpful to lay the words and explanations out in a multi-column chart to provide staff with a quick glance reminder (see table 2.1).[16]

Table 2.1.

USE . . .	INSTEAD OF . . .	BECAUSE . . .
Enslaved person, enslaved man/woman, enslaved laborer, enslaved maid, enslaved blacksmith, etc.	slave	Affirms personhood by recognizing a condition forced upon someone, rather than reducing them to a non-human noun.
Freedom Seeker or Self-Emancipator	runaway or fugitive	Acknowledges the agency of people striving to save their life, rather than defining them by a term that implies they were breaking the law by escaping an immoral and inhumane system forced upon them.

Brandon Dillard recalls the first time a student challenged him to explain an unfamiliar word that refers to a difficult concept.

> I remember well the first time I had a seven-year-old ask me, "what's a concubine?" I learned to shift my language quickly. . . . When talking about the relationship between Jefferson and Hemings, I often keep to the discourse of family and ownership. If they're very young, I simply say: "Jefferson had twelve children, six with his wife and six with a woman he owned, an enslaved woman named Sally Hemings.[17] We don't know much about her, not even how she felt about Thomas Jefferson, but we know her children grew up as slaves and weren't recognized by their father. He freed them when they became adults and then they moved far away to the North where slavery was illegal."[18]

At that point, Brandon can take the conversation in a couple of directions. With young students, he addresses the difficult choice of leaving one's family behind to start a new life. With older students he can have conversations about consent, or lack of it in the case of enslaved women.

> The [Thomas Jefferson] Foundation recognizes that the concept of consent in a master/slave relationship is an absurdity. Sally Hemings simply could not say no. But this does not mean we know anything about their feelings towards one another, and we make no claims or suppositions about those feelings. To do so denies Hemings the same agency she was denied in life, and we refuse to do that.[19]

Taking a lesson from Brandon's experience, it is important to assess one's language and word choice when developing your program.

What Is in a Name?

As you build an interpretive narrative, it is imperative to consider how you will address historical people in your stories. Will you only use honorifics (Mr./Mrs.) and titles (Dr./General) for white people? What about nicknames or diminutive names? How are you showing equal respect and humanity for historical people—Black and white? Consider this—is "Mammy" a respectful nickname an owner gave an enslaved woman because she cared for his children or is it a Jim Crow–diminutive stereotypically assigned to a woman who referred to herself, in her time, by her given/chosen name?

During a visit to Poplar Forest, Thomas Jefferson's personal retreat in western Virginia, I picked up on a disturbing pattern that was creating cognitive dissonance. The tour guide referred to the former president as "Mr. Jefferson" throughout the tour, as is standard for a site of this type. Inversely, he addressed John Hemmings, a skilled enslaved joiner and brother to Sally Hemings, as "Johnny" through the entire tour. I shuddered every time he said "Johnny." The informal name seemed way too disrespectful. To help allay my cognitive dissonance, I reached out to Dillard at Monticello. He said,

There are primary sources where Hemmings was referred to as Johnny, but those sources are [by] white masters reinforcing racial hierarchies using a system that infantilized people they owned through the subtle and pervasive power of language. Continuing their use is equally troubling, and I would say such usage can certainly be described as a microaggression (albeit implicit and likely unconscious). But it continues here and elsewhere through habit and implicit bias, and of course we are all guilty of some implicit biases. I see it as a call to work harder.[20]

John Hemmings was a literate and talented craftsman whom Jefferson entrusted with implementing his architectural designs at Poplar Forest. Hemmings signed his name as "John" in letters that he wrote to Jefferson family members, therefore I would encourage the use of the name he used to refer to himself. The constant diminution of Hemmings's name on the tour conveyed a lack of respect for his life and contributions.

At Mount Vernon, for years the staff referred to Washington's enslaved valet as "Billy Lee." But after a closer reading of Washington's will, and a willingness to raise the profile of those the Washingtons enslaved, the staff began using the name "William Lee." Curator Jessie McCloud explains,

Though the name "Billy Lee" appears frequently in popular histories and is well known, George Washington only referred to his valet by that diminutive until about 1771. After that date, Washington almost exclusively called him "Will" or "William." Compare Memorandum, List of Tithables, ca. June 14, 1771, *Papers of George Washington*, which lists "Billy" as a house servant; with Memorandum, List of Tithables, ca. June 10, 1772, *Papers of George Washington* (and subsequent lists), which record "Will." There is also evidence that William Lee himself preferred that name. In his will, Washington noted, "And to my Mulatto man William (calling himself William Lee) I give immediate freedom."[21]

The simple act of using an enslaved person's chosen name, rather than a diminutive, indicates respect for the personhood and their autonomy. Sites must meet this standard.

Similarly, at Royall House and Slave Quarters, the staff, and historians for more than two hundred years, referred to an African woman the Royalls enslaved simply as "Belinda." Her first petition for freedom in 1783 refers to her as "Belinda Royall," keeping with the common practice of calling enslaved people by the last name of their enslavers. However, in 2015 a new document came to light, a 1788 petition in which "she described herself as "Belinda Sutton of Boston in the County of Suffolk Widow."[22] We do not know who her husband was, or when they married, but we do know she signed as Belinda Sutton again in a 1793 petition. The staff now address her as Belinda Sutton.

As with the terminology of slavery, it is important to share with visitors why you chose to refer to people—both enslaved and free—with names and honorifics. If Monticello chooses to refer to Sally Hemings as "Miss Hemings," something that would not happen in her lifetime, the staff need to explain why they use that honorific to recognize her as more than just a first name. This helps visitors understand our rationale, allowing them to see historical thinking skills in action. The bottom line is that the words we use have deep meanings that convey dignity and respect, something nearly all people understand, including students.

Here are some additional concepts, adapted from Gloria Swindler Boutte and Jennifer Strickland's article "Making African American Culture and History Central to Early Childhood Teaching and Learning," that you might want to consider while developing a successful interpretive experience on the histories and legacies of slavery:[23]

- Incorporate information about the impact of African cultures on African American and American culture.
- Do not center African American history on slavery, but instead portray a robust picture of Africans and African-descended people in the context of U.S. and world history.
- Highlight the many independent nations, and diversely sophisticated people on the continent of Africa before, during, and after the slave trade era.
- Deconstruct typical historical accounts and address the moral issues of slavery.
- When discussing slavery within the context of other migration patterns, be sure to note it as "forced migration" not as "immigration."
- Portray neither white people nor Black people as being monolithic.
- Note that the concept of slavery manifested differently among other ethnic groups and nations throughout history.
- Use primary documents to make the stories come alive.

Change Is Hard, But Necessary and Possible

Rethinking values, goals, outcomes, and terminology involves realigning our programs about slavery. This will most likely disrupt your existing methodology. "We've always told the story this way." "Visitors won't like this." "This is revisionist history." I am pretty sure that every historic site or museum has heard one of these phrases—either verbatim or a version thereof. Success might mean giving up what you have always done (and possibly giving up on people too)—releasing old ways and adopting new ones. Yes, change is hard, but progress does not exist without it. It is important to foster those naysayers (board, staff, or volunteers) along in the process, but at some point, leadership must decide whether it is worth keeping people who impede or reject progress.

In 2007, the staff at Historic Fort Snelling in St. Paul, Minnesota, a property of the Minnesota Historical Society, began to comprehensively embrace the history of slavery at the fort, but this would mean a radical shift in how they did interpretation. The 150th anniversary of the Dred Scott decision spurred a broader look at slavery in the Minnesota territory. Dred Scott and his wife Harriet were enslaved at Fort Snelling between 1836 and 1840. They sued their enslaver since they had "lived as enslaved people in free territory at Fort Snelling and other places, and therefore should be granted their freedom."[24] It is a significant history that the institution had long ignored, choosing instead a moment-in-time, first-person interpretation of the year 1827, precluding the inclusion of the Scotts' story. After installing a static exhibit about the Scotts' life at Fort Snelling and their case for freedom, the staff realized that visitors wanted to talk about the story, so they added a staff

Figure 2.1.   A costumed interpreter leading a school group in the Dred and Harriett Scott quarters at Historic Fort Snelling, prior to the change in policy about historic costumes. Photo by Matt Cassady, courtesty of the Minnesota Historical Society.

person to the site. As their interpretation evolved, management realized that a predominantly white staff presenting in first person could not adequately interpret the lives of the Scotts and others enslaved at the fort. As Fort Snelling project manager Jeff Boorom shared, the fort's interpretive team—with input from consultants—decided the

> entire program [should be] switched to third person, not just the Scotts' space. The main costuming issue was staff comfort, [as] we were getting feedback they just weren't comfortable concentrating on slavery content while in costume. We also soon had African American staff that did not want to portray enslaved people as part of the living history program, but very much wanted to interpret slavery content. I think this also had an influence on the white staffs' discomfort with costuming in the space. We never really delved into why it was uncomfortable exactly. I believe we realized that costumed [white] staff occupying a place of enslavement was as problematic as consistency with any other program aesthetics, particularly in terms of appropriation of the narrative. It just didn't feel right.[25]

The summer of 2018 was the first summer that staff were not in costume in Fort Snelling's kitchen, where the combination of narratives—enslavement, domestic tasks, and hearth cooking—weighed most heavily on staff. Most of their concern surrounded the perception that by eliminating white women in period costume, the institution erased the physical representation of working-class women in the fort's history. "A big logistical issue," Boorom noted, "was continuing a hearth cooking program but without costuming. [It] didn't 'feel right' for some staff, [who] strongly associated with the 'living history' activity, but [couldn't do it] without the 'trappings.'"[26] Staff had so closely linked costumed interpretation to historic trades that they could not possibly imagine being able to demonstrate hearth cooking without a period dress on. Ultimately, management had to decide whether historic clothing was relevant if the main point of the program was to talk with visitors in third person. Also, with African American staff members wanting to interpret enslaved life at the fort but feeling uncomfortable about being in costume (and being ill-treated by visitors who regarded them as "slaves"), were the costumes necessary?

Even after extensive staff training, many remained unsure of the decision to eschew historical costumes. The management team decided it was important to clearly communicate to staff the motives and process for the no-costume decision. Their message read, in part, as follows:

> In the process of determining whether [white] staff would be costumed in [the kitchen], African American community members within the living history museum field were consulted, [and] the perspectives ranged from "white staff in costume (interpreting slavery) is a bad idea" to "white staff in costume is ok" to "don't have an opinion." [In] the final meeting where the decision was made, the main issue on the table was the ethical concern raised by all this, that we had to effectively address this concern if we chose to proceed with costuming. No counterpoints were made, so by default the decision was made to move away from costuming in this space. This all applies to the program in its entirety as we move[d] forward. [We should ask ourselves] what purpose is living history performing in any given aspect, how is it justifiable, how does its implementation effectively address ethical concerns brought forward by the communities directly invested. The fort [and the land it sits on] is sacred to multiple communities, [whites] included, and each of those communities holds multiple perspectives, often conflicting ones (in the same community). If a method-technic-approach to content doesn't serve a purpose and can't be "justified" while addressing concerns directly, it may not have a future in programming.[27]

Fort Snelling's management addressed staff and community member's concerns, while considering visitors' reservations. Most visitors—especially young people—find it easier to converse with a non-costumed staff member, particularly with a subject like slavery. Sometimes clothing presents an unspoken barrier between visitors and interpreters, as young people might feel intimidated or unsure of how to approach a costumed staff member. Will they respond in character or as if it is present day? An interpreter who insists on costumed interpretation because that is what *they* want to do is not engaging in learner-centered interpretation. When in doubt, or if you are not doing museum theater, clearly designated first-person interpretation, or a special demonstration set within historical context (and clearly communicated to the public), go without costumes.

I applaud the Fort Snelling staff for giving the time and resources, and consulting professionals outside of their organization, to make these important interpretive decisions. The change at Fort Snelling was not easy. Challenges remain and staff training is ongoing. Their process of revisiting their interpretive goals and thinking critically about the stories they want to tell forced them to redefine a successful experience, which involved giving up some long-lived (and loved) interpretive techniques to accommodate new techniques that make their stories accessible to a more diverse audience.

A lot of thoughtful work should go into laying the foundation for interpreting slavery with children and teens before you even start generating program ideas. Ensuring your organization is invested in its mission, vision, and values will create a strong base for program development. Determining your definition of a successful experience focuses your team as you chose pedagogy and interpretive techniques. Be aware, however, that you may have to be prepared to let some things go.

Notes

1. Samantha Cairns, "'Teaching' Challenging History," in *Challenging History in the Museum: International Perspectives*, ed. Jenny Kidd et al (London: Routledge, 2014), 196.
2. "Developing a Mission Statement, American Alliance of Museums, accessed April 6, 2019, https://www.aam-us.org/wp-content/uploads/2017/12/Developing-a-Mission-Statement-2018.pdf.
3. "Developing a Mission Statement."
4. "James Madison's Montpelier," accessed April 6, 2019, https://www.montpelier.org/about/foundation.
5. "Royall House and Slave Quarters," accessed March 17, 2019, http://www.royallhouse.org/about-us/mission-board-and-staff/.
6. Royall House and Slave Quarters' previous mission, dated December 2005, read, "The Royall House is a museum of national significance, operating as a cultural and educational resource for the general public. The Royall House Association is a membership organization open to all, dedicated to the preservation of the buildings and site and to the research and interpretation of the Royall House, particularly during the period when it was occupied by the Royall family."
7. "A Home for Brave Ideas," President Lincoln's Cottage, accessed January 19, 2018, http://www.lincolncottage.org/home-for-brave-ideas/.
8. "Historic Morven: A Window into America's Past," Morven Museum and Garden, accessed March 17, 2019, https://www.morven.org/permanent-exhibition-1.
9. Susan Nalezyty, email to the author, May 4, 2018.
10. Ywone D. Edwards-Ingram, *The Art and Soul of African American Interpretation* (Williamsburg, VA: Colonial Williamsburg Foundation, 2016), 71.
11. Janette Griffin, "The Museum Education Mix: Students, Teachers and Museum Educators," *Understanding Museums*, accessed January 19, 2018, http://nma.gov.au/research/understanding-museums/JGriffin_2011.html.
12. Jay McTighe and Grant Wiggins, *Understanding by Design* Framework, accessed July 6, 2018, http://www.ascd.org/ASCD/pdf/siteASCD/publications/UbD_WhitePaper0312.pdf.
13. "Telling Their Stories," Mount Vernon, tour observation, March 23, 2017.

14. Alan S. Marcus, Thomas H. Levine, and Robin S. Grenier, "How Secondary History Teachers Use and Think about Museums: Current Practices and Untapped Promise for Promoting Historical Understanding," *Theory & Research in Social Education* 40, no. 1 (2012): 72.

15. Richard Josey, conversation with the author, September 28, 2018.

16. Informed by an example from Kat Lloyd of the Tenement Museum, "Putting Essential Understanding/Foundational Truth into Practice" (online presentation, American Association for State and Local History conference, September 29, 2020).

17. The staff at Thomas Jefferson's Monticello spell Sally's last name with one *m*, the way that Jefferson spelled it, as there is no extant writing in her hand. Her brother, John Hemmings, spelled his name with two *m*'s. John was literate and always used two *m*'s.

18. Brandon Dillard, email to the author, May 13, 2019.

19. Brandon Dillard, email to the author, May 13, 2019.

20. Brandon Dillard, email to the author, February 24, 2019.

21. Jessie McCloud, "William (Billy) Lee," Mount Vernon Ladies Association, accessed August 4, 2018, https://www.mountvernon.org/library/digitalhistory/digital-encyclopedia/article/william-billy-lee.

22. "Belinda Sutton and Her Petitions," Royall House and Slave Quarters, accessed August 4, 2018, http://www.royallhouse.org/slavery/belinda-sutton-and-her-petitions/.

23. Adapted from Gloria Swindler Boutte and Jennifer Strickland, "Making African American Culture and History Central to Early Childhood Teaching and Learning," *The Journal of Negro Education* 77, no. 2 (Spring, 2008): 137.

24. "Enslaved African Americans and the Fight for Freedom," Minnesota Historical Society, accessed July 6, 2018, http://www.mnhs.org/fortsnelling/learn/african-americans.

25. Jeff Boorom, email to the author, July 6, 2018.

26. Jeff Boorom, email to the author, July 6, 2018.

27. Jeff Boorom, email to the author, June 7, 2018.

CHAPTER 3

Creating a Brave Space

> "I believe relevance unlocks new ways to build deep connections with people who don't immediately self-identify with our work. I believe relevance is the key to a locked room where meaning lives. We just have to find the right keys, the right doors, and the humility and courage to open them." —Nina Simon[1]

THE TOPIC of slavery is inherently uncomfortable for people of all ethnicities and many people may not always feel "safe" when discussing it. It can feel particularly "unsafe" for young people who do not have a robust scaffold of historical knowledge or the emotional maturity on which to hang these new narratives. First used in the 1960s in reference to the LGBT and women's movements, the term "safe space" referred to a physical, intellectual, and emotional space where like-minded people could share their thoughts and emotions without repercussions.[2] The wider world adopted the term as a standard concept for creating space for people to discuss any challenging topic. In recent years, academics have examined the term to acknowledge concerns that a space can never actually be completely "safe" for everybody. Mark Katrikh, director of operations and experiences at the Museum of Tolerance explains, "Museum professionals have recently shifted away from the term 'safe,' because it implies comfort, preferring to use other terms such as 'brave space.'"[3] Creating an emotionally safe space to talk about slavery may be difficult for museum educators due to the traumatizing nature of the content, but it is possible to establish a brave space in which we encourage students to be courageous in speaking up and sharing their thoughts about any manner of challenging content, helping them to make meaning.[4] I encourage museums and historic sites to consider the role of brave spaces in their programs, as the purpose of a brave space is to encourage dialogue while "recognizing difference and holding each person accountable to do the work of sharing experiences and coming to new understandings."[5]

Remember that it is important to revisit the purpose of your interpretation before developing any programming (see chapter 2). Do you want to tell students about history or enable them to learn from it? If your goal is for students to learn from and connect with the history, then you need to set up a brave space for them to dialogue—as learning happens best when people can talk through their thoughts. To paraphrase Minda Borun, former director of research and evaluation at the Franklin Institute, conversation *is* the currency of learning.[6] When establishing a brave space for conversation and learning about slavery, it is imperative students understand that ignorance (i.e., the lack of knowledge and not intentionally harmful ignorance) often accompanies the practice of bravery. In creating a brave space, all—staff and students—must be nonjudgmental and help each other. Making space for students to connect with the history, with their personal thoughts, and with each other, provides them the opportunity to be courageous, to challenge themselves and others to find relevance in the history, and take action to make change in their world.

Tips for Facilitating a Brave Space

Not everyone is prepared to jump into facilitating student dialogue. Training and gaining experience are important. (See chapter 8 for more on staff training.) Here are some basic tips to start:

1. Know how to be a facilitator. When talking with visitors about a challenging subject, it is important to know how to keep the conversation going in a positive direction. Learn good facilitation techniques (like the Arc of Dialogue) and practice them before going "live" with visitors.[7] As Mark Katrikh writes,

   > A practiced facilitator will blend into the background so as not in interfere with the process. If the goal is to not interfere but ask the right questions and allow the group to engage with the exhibits and each other, then one of the biggest challenges that disrupts this process are questions that are instantly identified as being difficult. For guides, these questions can cause involuntary intakes of breath and if not anticipated, a look of sheer terror. The beauty of facilitation is understanding that the techniques themselves absolve the guide of the need to be the expert.[8]

2. Be prepared and protect yourself. Find your center and your boundaries. Facilitating dialogue requires one to open up and share authentically, while keeping the focus on the content and the students, so be sure to know where your boundaries are. Guides, Katrikh argues,

   > cannot ask visitors to discuss very personal topics with each other without modeling such behavior for their group. As guides are asked to share of themselves, they must also take care of themselves. While much of the conversation around safety focuses on the group, guides must develop ways of coping with statements, comments, or reactions that impact them on a personal level such as an anti-gay slur spoken behind the back of the guide or an extreme political view espoused by a group participant. These types of comments have impact and cannot be easily dismissed. Museum staff must help guides be allies for each other and create avenues for reporting problems to management.[9]

3. Recognize that museums are not neutral. All museums and historic sites have a point of view or perspective on their topic, whether or not it is written or stated aloud. Your site is projecting its perspective about slavery based on how visible or invisible it is to your visitors. Sean Kelley, senior vice president and director of interpretation at Eastern State Penitentiary Historic Site explains that they removed "neutrality" from their mission because

> the word provided us an excuse for simply avoiding thorny issues of race, poverty, and policy that we weren't ready to address. . . . I thought neutrality would create a safe space for visitors, but it was becoming clear that this space wasn't safe for Americans who have experienced mass incarceration up close, within their communities. We have tried to shift our focus to effectiveness and inclusion. We have found that many leisure travelers really *will* engage with these difficult subjects, but core elements of museum craft become more important than ever. Experiences need to be social, multi-generational, interactive, and accessible to visitors who don't typically learn by reading alone. [Museums] need to genuinely value the wide perspectives and firsthand experiences of the visitors themselves.[10]

4. Get to know your audience. Doing this at the beginning of your time with the group helps build trust, which is essential to creating a brave space. Our time with our visitors is limited; however, by taking time to ask your students a few introductory questions you can show them that you are interested in them and what they have to say. If students feel that you have a genuine interest in them, and they feel like the guide is invested in what they have to say, the dialogue will be much more impactful. For a school group, in addition to knowing where they are from, you might ask them what they have been studying in school and what they know about your site that might connect to their curriculum. You might want to ask them what questions they have about your topic/site, as this will give you an idea of their knowledge base and what they are interested in exploring.

5. Acknowledge the content is inherently uncomfortable and emotionally triggering. Some students will ask questions out of innocent ignorance, not knowing or intending their comments as hurtful. A student may also intentionally say something that is triggering or harmful. As Katrikh notes,

> When a student asks a question, particularly one that is rooted in some sort of trauma or can be interpreted as difficult or contradictory in nature, the guide's affirmation of the questioner begins the process of addressing the question. A simple statement such as "I appreciate your willingness to raise these issues" from the guide will begin to put the group at ease and allow for productive conversation to follow. Heightened emotional states often require a simple acknowledgment to defuse the emotion. If the question is not fully formed, follow-up questions or a restatement of the question can provide clarity. The guide can then move the conversation to a universal theme that allows for multiple perspectives and the input

of other members of the group. This is a strategy to help reframe the issue for the group to move the conversation to "safer" ground. It also eliminates a situation where the guide and questioner find themselves in a back-and-forth discussion to the exclusion of other group members.[11]

6. Be aware of group dynamics. School groups arrive at your site with preset social relationships, as many of them have known each other for years. You, the tour guide, are the unknown factor. Take a few minutes to get to know the group (see number three on this list). Observe them, who is the talkative one, the outgoing one, the quiet one. Identify subgroups and strategize how you might use those dynamics to the group's benefit and engage them all in the experience. Katrikh observes,

> Group members' reactions can run the gamut from benign or no interest to extreme agitation and can be triggered by the first question and/or the response of the guide. It is incumbent upon the guide to be aware of group dynamics and the individual reactions of group members and respond accordingly. Sometimes groups react to the question asked . . . other times the reaction has to do with pre-existing relationships within the group. The group may take offense or dismiss comments from a member if there is a history of that person talking too much or asking other inappropriate questions. The guide may appreciate having someone regularly respond to their prompts without realizing that each interaction annoys the rest of the group members. Sometimes, there is an underlying deference to the questioner, who may outrank the other group members or may have some other status that is not readily visible. If these relationships exist and are somehow impacting interaction, then guides may have to utilize a completely distinct set of tools regarding group dynamics to address the issue.[12]

7. Establish ground rules for your discussions. The inherent emotional nature of the content necessitates reminding student visitors that we need to be both "head smart" and "heart smart" about ourselves and others. Slavery is a tough subject and talking about it should be both intellectual and emotional. Students want to understand the history and assimilate it into what they already know—and the topic touches on the highest highs and lowest lows of our emotions. We must be aware that some people will have deep emotional connections with the content, which may manifest themselves in various physical and verbal reactions. Here is an example of some ground rules I use in my workshops:[13]

- Seek first to understand, then to be understood.[14]
- Be open to different perspectives and feelings and be honest about your own.
- We have a brief time together. Share the "airtime." Speak from your own experience.
- Be willing to examine your own assumptions and feel free to change your mind.

- Respect the confidentiality of the group.
- It is okay to be "raggedy," meaning you can talk through your thoughts without having to grasp just the right words to express what you are thinking.[15]

Katrikh notes, "These ground rules will often try to preempt any misunderstanding by stating outright that group members may be triggered at any point in the experience and should focus on the intent of the speakers rather than on a trigger word. While this will not prevent a conflict from arising, a quick reference back to those guidelines can help deflate the conflict."[16]

8. Check yourself. Interpretation is an experience you build together. A museum or historic site tour is not about you (the guide), it is about your visitors. Resist the urge to share your opinions or unload all the information you know. Instead focus on helping your visitors build an understanding of the historical content. Katrikh notes,

> Museum staff must ensure that guides are striking a balance between sharing why they are passionate about a subject without overwhelming the experience with their own stories and anecdotes. Moreover, if those stories and anecdotes specifically contradict museum content visitors can be confused. This can be particularly tricky for guides who bring their own personal experience with the events covered in the museum. People have their own opinions and are prone to sharing them. Guides who bring their own political opinions to the conversation undermine the safety of the group and can contradict the values of the museum itself. Since most museum content is inherently political, to insist on a non-political environment and deny reality is to appear disingenuous. However, engaging in nonpartisan conversation and allowing many disparate opinions to enter the discussion, will uphold the value of facilitation and only heighten the experience of the visitor.[17]

9. Your content connects globally. We must recognize that the story of African chattel slavery in America did not start in 1619 and end in 1865, and that white Americans did not have a monopoly on evil when it came to oppressing and dehumanizing people of color. The African slave trade was a multinational, economic juggernaut that affected, and continues to affect, millions of people around the world. The Black Lives Matter movement is a direct descendent of the Civil Rights Movement and anti-slavery activists. Per Katrikh,

> [The] events happening in the outside world absolutely impact the conversation inside the museum. Conversely, the conversations that take place in the museum must be linked to global events and have the potential to impact the world outside the museum walls. . . . Focusing on global impact allows the conversations to transcend the specific discussions taking place and connect to more universal themes. Rather than allowing visitors to leave with the impression that the events discussed affected other people in another time and place, they need to leave with

an understanding of how the past impacts the present and future, and that they can participate in shaping our world.[18]

Connect by Showing Respect

At a Juneteenth event at Boston's Museum of Fine Arts, a celebration to commemorate the end of slavery, I heard an artist proclaim, "A space cannot be safe until you recognize the humanity of everyone in it."[19] This struck me to be true to our work. We must show respect for and see the humanity in ALL our student visitors so that they may feel accepted and brave. I saw firsthand how one adept educator created a brave space for students to have a challenging conversation about slavery in New Hampshire. At the Moffatt-Ladd House in Portsmouth, the eighteenth-century home of the William Whipple family and enslaved men Prince Whipple and Windsor Moffatt, Keith Mascoll, an African American actor and educator, adeptly moved the all-white student group into a discussion about how slavery—particularly race and class—affect their lives today. Mascoll did this by employing some simple and effective behaviors:

1. Build a group culture on an even playing field by telling them there is no right or wrong answers to the questions. Give students honesty and respect and expect it in return.
2. Share information about yourself, where relevant, and be vulnerable.
3. Do not talk down to them. Talk *with* them and try to involve everyone.
4. Note that we are in this [this discussion and this world] together. (He not only expresses this verbally but by "the energy I have in my body.")
5. Empower the young people to talk. Tell them, "I really want to hear what you have to say."
6. Change the normal dynamic of just hearing from certain people by asking others to contribute—to be heard and seen. (After the program, he often hears from the classroom teacher that there were kids who never talk in the classroom that felt comfortable participating in the conversation.)
7. Establish that everybody's voice is equal. Say, "I need to hear from other people."
8. The presenter's body language is key. Be sure that your physical cues do not bely the equality you are trying to establish.
9. Thank each student for their comment. Do not express any judgement. Follow up with questions to clarify if you are not sure what the student means.
10. Do not get in the way! It is not all about the facilitator. Foster the dialogue among students, not just between you and them.[20]

Sometimes the inevitable does happen, a student makes a comment or asks a question that sucks the air out of the room. When I was observing Mascoll's program at the Moffatt-Ladd House, one student commented that her brother (a white boy of middle school age) had experienced "reverse racism" from a Black man on a recent visit to Washington, DC.

Mascoll followed up on the student's comment with some questions to help her dig a bit deeper into why she thought and said what she did:

- What does "reverse racism" look like?
- Why does the term "reverse" apply in this situation?
- What were the signs that it was happening?
- How does that make you feel?
- What do you think should be done about it?
- Did anything change in the context and status of his life when he experienced that "reverse racism?" Why or why not?

Simple questions like these help students unpack their thoughts and feelings about how race and racism play out in their lives, without being threatening or judgmental. "Children struggle with bias and stereotypes," Linda Blanshay writes, "because they learned it from the adults and social world around them. Research on prejudice in children has shown that their impressions of 'the other' mirror the social structures that, while unspoken, are clearly visible to all. . . . Social justice education then involves naming and critically analyzing these structures."[21]

As Mascoll demonstrated by creating a caring, respectful environment, students can be empowered to ask and answer difficult questions and talk through their learning crisis as they integrate new information with old.[22]

Connect through Personal Empowerment

I noticed a trend as I observed school programs at the different museums and historic sites where I did my research. Students connected more to the past when the guide talked about the agency students have today (their ability to take deliberate actions) and encouraged them to take lessons from the enslaved and free African Americans of the past and apply it to their own lives. I saw several tour guides, of various identities, make these connections. The guides I observed identified as African American men (three), African American woman (one), white men (two), and white women (four). One-third of the group leaders were African American, and the tone that they set for the program was often different— not better or worse, just different—from their white colleagues. At the Frederick Douglass National Historic Site, I followed tours by both white and African American male rangers. Each was a solid tour, but each ranger took a different approach to creating a brave space and helping the students to connect Douglass to their lives.

After the tour by Ranger John, an African American man, the students made statements of personal empowerment on their post-visit evaluations, noting the following: "It was meant for us to carry on our ancestors' past. That means to me that I could be the future the country needs" and "They said that we were the future of tomorrow, and that motivated me to keep doing my best."[23] Ranger John used storytelling to emphasize the importance of education to Douglass's life and accomplishments. He selected objects in each room that prompted stories about Douglass's life. He invited students into a dialogue about the use of violence to make a point, asking, "When is it okay to use violence?" Ranger John left plenty of room for questions from the students, using their natural inquisitiveness as a strategy to build personal relevance. He also made the conscious decision to connect stories of Douglass's agency to stories of agency in his (John's) own life. He also encouraged students to find ways to exercise their own agency, thus establishing a brave space by giving students a chance to talk and find their own relevance to Douglass's life.

In contrast, Ranger Nate, a white man, focused his tour on how Douglass fought the stereotype of an uneducated, unclean, and ignorant enslaved man. Nate told the students that through his eloquent oratory and fashionable sartorial choices, Douglass set a new standard for how free African Americans could exist in the white world of the late nineteenth century. Like John, Nate also used objects and photographs of Douglass to initiate stories about the abolitionist leader's life and offer students a vision of their potential to make change. Student responses directly addressed Douglass's legacy as an abolitionist leader and its connections to their lives today:

- "The guide made me feel like I could do anything, that I am the future as long as I put myself into it."
- "It meant a lot to talk about my future and what it means."
- "At the end of the tour he summed up how you can overcome great obstacles with determination."
- "We are the future."
- "How our choices now affect us later. It's motivational."[24]

While Nate and John approached the tour from slightly different angles, they each created a space for students to discuss how they felt about Douglass's life and its relevance today, thus enabling them make connections to their own lives. Neither followed a rigid tour outline, instead they had a goal in mind and were flexible about how they got there. Each had a distinct style that allowed students to participate in the meaning making. They demonstrated what the "Challenging History Summary Document" called, "a space within educational programs to more fully engage with the challenges of such a history . . . ; education programs can be far more flexible. Educational programs should engage more fully with multiple narratives, provide more challenging frames, provoke dialogue and even engage emotionally."[25]

As we more holistically engage students intellectually and emotionally, museums and historic sites must consider the changes they want to encourage in their students' lives. Visitors should not remain unchanged after engaging in this challenging content and it is our obligation to consider how to effectively channel those changes. For example, decisions about content and methodology at the Museum of Tolerance in Los Angeles are based on what Katrikh calls

the idea that the purpose of the museum was to allow visitors to learn from history, not to teach about historic events. Moving visitors to a place where they would be motivated to act in the world around them required an understanding of the interconnectivity of history and its impact today.[26]

How do you see your school programs facilitating change in students' lives? We can foster lessons of change on all levels. History is rife with stories of individual agency, but it can be scary to think of putting one's self out there alone. Collective action is just as empowering and powerful, as Tema Okun notes in *The Emperor Has No Clothes: Teaching Race and Racism to People Who Don't Want to Know*, a "collective of persons are capable of actions and understandings that transcend individuals on their own."[27] It is imperative to change our expectations of the power of interpretation to help students see how history matters to their future.

Connect through Identity

One way to engage students in conversation together and with historical actors is through identity characteristics. If you want to move slowly into a brave space, ask students to consider their own identity before broaching the subject of slavery. (Because who doesn't like to talk about themselves?) You can start by asking students to think about what makes up their identities. This includes their social or external-facing identity (skin color, presenting gender, age, physical characteristics) and their personal or internal identity characteristics (beliefs, values, personality traits) that are less visible to others. These identities can be individual (your place in your family's birth order) and/or collective (being a Girl Scout). Both create a larger sense of belonging or representation. Once you have discussed the different facets of identity, ask students to create a list of their identities, making sure to include the personal and social, individual and group aspects. Ask for volunteers to share their words and how those identities make them the person they are.

After you have laid this groundwork, break them into groups to discuss the profiles of people enslaved at your site. Here is how the activity would unfold using this profile of Wilson, a man enslaved at Mount Vernon:

> Wilson was the oldest son of Caroline Branham, a house maid, and Peter Hardiman, a groom. Wilson helped his father feed, brush, and exercise the horses at Mansion House Farm. He also rode one of the horses that pulled Washington's carriages. Wilson was fourteen or fifteen when he led George Washington's rider-less horse in the general's funeral procession on December 18, 1799.[28]

Ask students to highlight Wilson's social and personal identity characteristics. (They may have to do some extrapolating to come up with some personal identities.) In Wilson's case, students might call out his identities as male, son, brother, oldest son, enslaved, likes animals, attentive to detail, rides horses well, takes pride in work, born in Virginia, has a mom and dad, and African American.

Next ask students to compare their own identity lists to those they made for Wilson. Ask them to look for similarities or differences between their own identities and Wilson's, and then ask them to draw conclusions about their shared identities. By connecting through identity characteristics, students can begin to open up and share (there's no "wrong" answer to what makes up your own identity), foster empathy for others, and see enslaved people as human beings.

While the topic of slavery can be intellectually challenging and emotionally charged for our student visitors, providing them with a brave space is essential for promoting dialogue and finding personal relevance. Establishing a brave space for students is predicated on each staff member individually, and as an institution collectively, doing the work to explore their relationship with race, sharpen their dialogue facilitation skills, and be confident in their ability to empower or ease students' emotions. When you treat your students with respect, they feel valued and open up to you and their classmates. Immersing your students in a brave space will take their learning to a whole new level of understanding and connection.

Notes

1. Nina Simon, "The Art of Relevance," June 27, 2016; accessed September 27, 2020, http://www .artofrelevance.org/2016/06/27/introduction-unlocking-relevance/.
2. Malcom Harris, "What's a 'Safe Space'? A Look at the Phrase's 50-Year History," November 11, 2015; accessed June 30, 2018, https://splinternews.com/what-s-a-safe-space-a-look-at -the-phrases-50-year-hi-1793852786.
3. Mark Katrikh, "Creating Safe(r) Spaces for Visitors and Staff in Museum Programs," *Journal of Museum Education* 43, no.1 (2018): 8.
4. "A *safe space* is ideally one that doesn't incite judgment based on identity or experience—where the expression of both can exist and be affirmed without fear of repercussion and without the pressure to educate. While learning may occur in these spaces, the ultimate goal is to provide support. A *brave space* encourages dialogue. Recognizing difference and holding each person accountable to do the work of sharing experiences and coming to new understandings—a feat that's often hard, and typically *uncomfortable*. We'd be remiss to simply hear the new term *brave space* and throw the old one out like a mistake we'd like to quickly forget. The reality is: they're different spaces, providing different outcomes." From, "Do We Need Safe Spaces or Brave Spaces?" Break Away, December 1, 2017; accessed February 2, 2021, https://alternative breaks.org/safe-or-brave-spaces/#:~:text=A%20safe%20space%20is%20ideally,without%20 the%20 pressure%20to%20educate.&text=A%20brave%20space%20encourages%20dialogue.
5. "Do We Need Safe Spaces or Brave Spaces?"
6. Minda Borun, presentation to the staff of USS Constitution Museum, 2005.
7. For more information on the Arc of Dialogue: https://mylearning.nps.gov/library-resources/ arc-of-dialogue-strategy/.
8. Katrikh, "Creating Safe(r) Spaces," 10.
9. Katrikh, "Creating Safe(r) Spaces," 10.
10. Sean Kelley, "Beyond Neutrality," *Center for the Future of Museums* (blog), August 23, 2016; accessed February 18, 2019, https://www.aam-us.org/2016/08/23/beyond-neutrality/.
11. Katrikh, "Creating Safe(r) Spaces," 11.
12. Katrikh, "Creating Safe(r) Spaces," 12.
13. Some of these tips were adapted from a workshop conducted by the International Coalition of Sites of Conscience.

14. Franklin Covey, "Habit 5: Seek First to Understand, Then to Be Understood," accessed September 20, 2020, https://www.franklincovey.com/the-7-habits/habit-5.html.

15. Shared by Raynetta Jackson-Clay, director of student activities at Georgetown Visitation Preparatory School, during a workshop.

16. Katrikh, "Creating Safe(r) Spaces," 12.

17. Katrikh, "Creating Safe(r) Spaces," 13.

18. Katrikh, "Creating Safe(r) Spaces," 14.

19. Des Polk, "The City Talks: Sharing Black Histories," Juneteenth event at Museum of Fine Arts Boston, June 19, 2019.

20. Keith Mascoll, interview with the author, May 25, 2018.

21. Linda Blanshay, "Talking about Immigration with Children through a Social Justice Lens," in *Interpreting Immigration at Museums and Historic Sites,* ed. Dina Bailey (Lanham, MD: Rowman and Littlefield, 2018), 59.

22. Jenny Kidd, "Challenging History Summary Document," accessed June, 13, 2021, https://www.city.ac.uk/_data/assets/pdf_file/0004/84082/Challenging-History-Summative-Document.pdf.

23. Student feedback from post-visit surveys at Frederick Douglass National Historic Site, March 30, 2017.

24. Student feedback from post-visit surveys at Frederick Douglass National Historic Site, March 30, 2017.

25. Kidd, "Challenging History Summary Document."

26. Katrikh, "Creating Safe(r) Spaces," 7.

27. Tema Okun, *The Emperor Has No Clothes: Teaching Race and Racism to People Who Don't Want to Know* (Charlotte, North Carolina: Information Age Publishing, Inc. 2010), 123.

28. Linda Powell, email to the author, February 26, 2018.

CHAPTER 4

What Is Age Appropriate?

"It is easier to build strong children than to repair broken men." —Frederick Douglass

ALL TOO often I encounter adults in workshops who tell me, "That's not what I learned about slavery in school," or "Why didn't anyone tell me this when I was young?" For decades, schools and museums have obscured and neglected our collective history of slavery, creating generations of people who have false or incomplete understandings of slavery and the people it affected. This has been one of the driving forces in perpetuating racial discord and false racial dichotomies. In response to Douglass's quote, museums and historic sites must now be at the vanguard of building intellectually and emotionally aware children, providing an accurate history of slavery, and supporting students with age-appropriate tools to discuss and process it.

Omission Is Oppression

There are many reasons slavery has remained in the margins of formal and informal education in the United States, including a lack of accurate knowledge, a denial of the existence of systemic racism, a desire to "get past it" because it happened a long time ago, and a wish (on the part of parents and educators) to protect children from the difficulties and horrors of life. (It is ironic that the desire to shield young people from all manner of human evil does not seem to stop us from encouraging kids to play war through pretend militia drills at historic sites or telling them terrifying stories of innocent women being hanged as witches.) These rationales are inexcusable and harmful to student development. Luckily, there is a remedy for them.

Lying about our history by omitting stories of slavery perpetuates the oppression of African Americans past and present and hinders students' ability to understand the agency and humanity of the same. Kids value honesty and often see right through the smoke screens adults assemble to protect them. Slavery has a long and complex history in the

United States, and it is not possible for one program, field trip, or tour to cover it all. But it is important to introduce all young visitors, no matter the age, to the topic at age-appropriate levels. It is imperative for museums to step forward, not only as the integrity-bound organizations we profess to be, but as the truth-telling, historically comprehensive, and future-looking organizations we *must be* to maintain relevance with twenty-first-century audiences.

How Kids Understand Historical Time

Before addressing the interpretation of slavery by age and developmental level, it is important to understand that the basic concept of history—events happening over the passage of time—is incomprehensible to very young visitors. While even children as young as five can learn about the concept of slavery, they lack a frame of reference for periods of time. It is useless to give them the traditional benchmarks like "before the Civil War" or "after the Pilgrims." Not until about ages seven, eight, or nine do children begin to really understand the concept of sequential historical time. Using terminology such as "a long time ago" or "way back before your grandparents were born" is appropriate with kids under nine years old. This helps them grasp the concept that what you are talking about is not happening now. As Stephen J. Thornton and Ronald Vukelich write, "The past-present dichotomy can be introduced any time after four years of age . . . [and] persons or events of the past should be introduced and discussed without dates prior to age nine."[1] Children between ages nine and eleven still use these general terms but can grasp the concept of a sequence of time a bit more (e.g., the Civil War came before World War II). Pre-teens and teens can start using specific dates and times in accurate order, with older adolescents' understanding of time approximating that of adults.[2]

Developmental Stages and Grade Levels

Before you start developing school or family programs, do some research into your intended audience. The fields of child psychology and developmental learning stages are deep and there are many books available about age—and grade-level—appropriateness, including *Education Psychology* by Anita Woolfolk[3] and *Yardsticks: Childhood and Adolescent Development Ages 4–14* by Chip Wood.[4] As you consult these sources, learn about the cognitive, physical, and social/emotional development of that age group. This provides insight into how they learn and what they have the capacity to understand.

In addition to researching the developmental capabilities of the age group, conduct some front-end evaluation. A focus group of teachers, and their students, is a good place to start. You will probably want to know the following:

- What does this age group already know and understand about slavery?
- What do they want to know?
- What are their frames of reference for understanding slavery? When do these references expand or change?

- When and how is slavery introduced and expanded on in school?
- What is an adult's role in supporting and extending children's engagement and understanding of slavery?[5]

Answers to these and other questions will help create a solid foundation for your program development work.

While looking at the literature and talking with the teachers, think about how the developmental characteristics of each age group will affect how you frame your narratives. Below, I have assembled some descriptions of age-specific developmental characteristics and ways you might apply them to your interpretation of slavery.

Early Childhood (Ages 4–6)

Children are smart, observant, and intuitive beings. They learn by using their senses to take in the world around them. Kids soak up the behavior and language that adults model for them. If a child sees that talking about slavery makes adults uncomfortable, they learn to avoid the subject. It is not wise to begin with the horrors of slavery with very young children. Instead, start with a subject that youngsters know a lot about—themselves! Anna Forgerson Hindley describes early childhood programs at the National Museum of African American History and Culture (NMAAHC) as following a simple process to help children make connections:

> [Start] with the individual child by empowering them to identify a positive identity trait (i.e., "I am kind, I am brave," etc.), using an object that tells a story related to that trait, and then to make connections with other people, whether in history or the other children in that room, to find similarities. Then we look at how even in the ways we are the same (loving, smart, etc.) we do things in different ways. We are all the same. We are all different. Isn't it wonderful![6]

The NMAAHC staff also use the concept of choices to frame their early childhood programs. They want children to realize that we constantly make choices that define us, that impact others, and that can define a nation, but that someone who was enslaved did not have the power to make choices for themselves or their family.

Young children respond best to the themes that are realities in their own lives, like fairness and community. "The way they understand these themes at three or thirteen is different, but humans are always gaining understanding in real time and that's what's defining them as people," Hindley noted.[7] From a very young age, children comprehend the concept of fairness. It is possible to explain to a four-year-old that slavery in the United States meant that people from Africa were taken from their homes and families and forced to work long hours doing hard work without being paid, and they were unable to make any significant choices about their lives. Most young children understand that it is not fair to be removed from your family, to have the ability to make choices taken away, or to not be compensated for hard work.[8] Share with students the true story of an enslaved family being separated and ask them what they think about it or what emotions came up for them. This will help youngsters start to form empathetic connections with people from the past.

Figure 4.1. Historical interpreter Dontavius Williams uses material culture to teach a young family member about slavery by allowing him to handle a brick made by an enslaved brickmaker. The young visitor places his thumb in the thumbprint of the brickmaker. Courtesy of Dontavius Williams, owner of The Chronicles of Adam.

Dr. Beverly Daniel Tatum suggests using picture books to begin conversations about slavery and opposing injustice.[9] Well-written, age-appropriate children's literature is a fantastic way to expose young people to simplified versions of the harsh realities of history, followed by an opportunity to process their thoughts and feelings about what they just heard or read. You might read the book at the beginning of the program to set up the narrative, or to use the story to motivate a discussion at different tour stops.

There are many children's books on slavery, some better than others, so here are a few tips on selecting a good one.

- The narrative balances the horrors of the institution of slavery (beatings, separation from family, loss of freedoms, etc.) with stories of agency—self-emancipation, mastery of a trade, marriage by choice, family ties, and so forth.
- The book tells the story of a real enslaved person.
- The author does not "sugarcoat" the institution of slavery or perpetuate mythology. For example: good masters, the overwhelming privilege of working in the big house, happy slaves, and so on.
- The narrative discusses what is happening to enslaved people and why.

Books such as *Henry's Freedom Box*[10] and *My Name Is James Madison Hemings*[11] offer young people a glimpse of the difficulties enslaved people faced, as well as the humanizing aspects of their lives, their emotions, their families, their cultural traditions, and the like. It is essential to conclude *all* student programs, but especially those for the youngest ones, with a discussion of the stories of agency, of deliberate action, and achievement in African American history. You could use the aforementioned identity exercise with a book: students list their positive identity traits and compare them with the identity traits of an enslaved person portrayed in a children's book. This is a great way for kids to see the humanity of those who were enslaved.

Children this age love to play dress-up and pretend to do chores; however, in the context of the history of slavery, these teaching techniques pose some serious concerns. I will address these further, along with more on the concept of fostering empathy, in chapters 5 and 6.

Elementary School (Ages 6–10)

Elementary-age students are curious and open to learning additional information. They can also detect dishonesty and may resent adults that do not tell the truth or omit parts of the story. They are at the perfect age to start unraveling the stories surrounding America's long history with slavery and its aftermath. "It's complicated. It's nuanced. It's uncomfortable and painful," Richard Josey notes. "Yet, it is ingrained in the DNA of the American identity. We need our future citizens to understand the inextricable connection between the past, the present, and the future."[12] We have long considered elementary school students old enough to learn concepts of patriotism and good citizenship, then they are also mature enough to learn why those qualities are so valuable and how our country has not always afforded them to all people.

While young students are also eager to share and make connections between the content and their own lives, they are also less practiced than adults in doing so in a manner that is considerate of others' feelings and emotions. Thus, you must begin discussions about slavery with ground rules about what it means to be respectful to each other and to historical actors. You might ask students what "being respectful" means, and what that looks like with a classmate or an adult. Then translate their answers into what it means to be respectful of the history—as you will be talking about real people who had thoughts and feelings. Tell students they must speak of historical people with carefully chosen words, and that they must support their opinions with evidence and explanation. For example, it is not okay for a student to say, "George Washington was a bad man because he owned slaves." Students must explain their thinking behind calling him "bad." Have them cite historical evidence or explain what they saw or heard that leads them to that conclusion.

Here are some tips for framing of slavery for elementary students:

- Contextualize slavery in themes like diversity, courage, and activism as an entrée into nuanced discussions about specific enslaved people.
- Notice students' discomfort and acknowledge it. Let them know that this is normal. You can say, "It is hard to talk about slavery. It can make some people feel bad.

Sometimes I feel _____." You can fill in the blank yourself. Let them know that feelings of guilt or anger are common.[13]

- Let students see themselves as agents of change and healing. Although slavery ended a long time ago, we still face racism today. By treating one another with respect, students are fighting racism.[14]

- Encourage them to note examples of bias and stereotypes, which is especially important, so they examine their home life and the world around them. Children can learn to question whether derogatory depictions of other people are stereotypes. They can interrogate a story to find out who are the "actors" and why; who is in the role of leader and who is taking the orders; and who has been left out of the story altogether.[15]

Pre- and post-visit surveys of fourth graders at Historic London Town in Edgewater, Maryland, revealed how much the students processed about the institution of slavery during their visit.[16] In the survey, I asked students the same question before and after the program: "What do you think are the two or three most important things to know about slavery?" Their pre-visit surveys cited very generic facts about slavery, "Slavery was bad," "Abraham Lincoln ended it," "Slaves escaped using the underground railroad," and "They were poor." Post-visit responses reflected a much more human-centric, nuanced understanding of slavery. "Once a baby is born to an enslaved person, they automatically become a slave," "Some slaves like Bet were taken from their families," "Slaves worked for their owners and didn't get paid. Indentured servants were poor people who didn't have money for a trip, but had to have someone rich pay," and "Some of the slaves don't have last names because they were separated from their parents."

What had happened between the pre- and post-visit surveys that led to a more human-centric understanding of slavery? The tour guide invoked stories about several different enslaved people, including the aforementioned Bet. These stories included details of the jobs enslaved people performed, as well as emotional stories about family separation. Through these narratives, students were able to process, at their developmental level, what it meant to be enslaved in an early eighteenth-century maritime community.

Like most young people, elementary-age students need to move around a lot. Try not to fight it as it is a natural developmental characteristic, and do not keep them sitting or standing still in one place for too long. Resist the urge to do what I observed at one site with a fifth-grade school program. The museum staff first sat students in uncomfortable plastic chairs to view a thirty-minute PowerPoint presentation. Students remained in the same seats for an activity related to archaeological finds unearthed during an excavation of the slave quarters. As interesting as the content was, it was way too long for them to be sitting in one place and students got restless and bored. More importantly, it made the learning of the content that much more difficult. Perhaps the PowerPoint could have been delivered by the classroom teacher as a pre-visit lesson, with a brief refresher at the beginning of their visit. This would have relieved students' time in the seats and allowed them more time to explore the house and artifacts.

One strategy often employed at historic sites with students of this age is the scavenger hunt. This keeps them moving, which is good for the developmental level, and they can cover a lot of intellectual, and physical, ground. When done well, with the assistance of competent chaperones, scavenger hunts are a somewhat effective strategy. But all too often institutions use this strategy to avoid going in-depth about the challenging history of slavery, or to move as many kids through a site as possible.

In 2015 I picked up a copy of an upper elementary version of a scavenger hunt from the Aiken-Rhett House, a Historic Charleston Foundation property. This document asked students to explore the house and check off the correct answers to questions about the house and people who lived in it. Some of the questions mentioning slavery included the following:

- "Urban house slaves could have to work at all hours of the day. *True or False*"
- "The agriculture-based economy of South Carolina was dependent on the labor of the enslaved Africans. *True or False*"
- "Which of the following is a cultural contribution of the Gullah people in Charleston? *Music, Art, Language, Crafts, Food, Stories, Clothing or All of the Above*"[17]

While the activity attempts to address the jobs of enslaved people and to acknowledge the contributions of Gullah (a community of enslaved Africans, and their descendants, in South Carolina/Georgia who share cultural characteristics with the people of Sierra Leone) to the wider Charleston community, the over-simplification of the content is unsettling. Questions and statements should ask students to think critically about slavery. For example, instead of a true/false statement about the hours an urban enslaved person worked, students might instead be asked to read about the experiences of a person enslaved at the Aiken's Charleston home and look closely at historical evidence in a room and respond by generating questions to ask the "urban enslaved person" about his or her life. This reinforces the notion that the enslaved were actual *people* and encourages students to be invested in an enslaved person's life. An activity like this also moves students away from checking boxes and gets them to engage with what they are seeing.

Middle School (Ages 10–13)

Educators might have a negative impression about middle schoolers because they often appear bored or disengaged. On the contrary, it is a fascinating age in which students are old enough to start integrating knowledge and themselves into the wider world. We need to stop treating middle school groups as burdens and move away from our negative biases about them.

Research shows that "a young adolescent brain can [only] hold seven items of information, plus or minus two items, in working memory."[18] Too often educators try to cram a bunch of content into their students' heads and middle schoolers are not able to process it fast enough, so they might disengage or glaze over while trying to assimilate it all into their existing knowledge. There is no need to overload students with information. They will not retain it, and they will have a hard time finding relevance in all the content coming at them. Build your program around a theme, share a piece of content related to that theme, and allow students time to process and connect to the content. Starting in sixth grade, students develop a more sophisticated sense of empathy and can address larger concepts like justice in a more holistic way. We should lean into that and encourage them to explore, and respond to, injustices of the past and present.

Humans are social animals, especially middle schoolers, so why not play to that strength. The brain requires interactions with other humans to properly develop.[19] Please, please, please, do not expect your students to come to your site and listen to a long house tour. No matter how engaging the speaker, no matter how interesting the scavenger hunt, or how many open-ended questions you ask, making middle school students sit and be quiet or fill in a worksheet is akin to a learning desert. Build pair-and-share, group discussion, or other collaborative learning opportunities into your programs.

Adolescent thinking is different from adult thinking. The gray matter in their brains is still forming. Many pre-teens are of the mistaken impression they think like and should be treated like adults, but adolescents make decisions based on feelings rather than logical thought processing.

There are two factors that strongly influence whether their brain pays attention to a piece of information: if the information has meaning and the information causes an emotional response.[20] Therefore, when developing programs for students of this age group, show respect for their thoughts while helping them find the emotional connection or relevance to their own lives. The content has to mean something to them or they simply will not care about it. They must be able to emotionally connect to the content, even though they might not outwardly express an emotion.

I saw the blending of emotional connection and storytelling with a group of African American and Hispanic eighth graders during a field trip to the Frederick Douglass National Historic Site in Washington, DC. The tour guide, Ranger John (see chapter 3), consistently made connections to Douglass's life, the modern Civil Rights Movement, and today's Black Lives Matter. He brought Douglass to life by talking about him as an ordinary man who took charge of his life to change his circumstances and fight for what he believed in. John also shared inspirational stories from his own life as a lesson of how people can rise above their circumstances to achieve. In their post-visit survey, students shared what they found relevant during the tour:

- "When he told us [that] we can be the next doctor or whatever we want to do just by learning and staying focused."
- "The ranger at Frederick's house said that we young people can do anything in life to be successful. We are all 'talented.' Which made me feel like somebody who can do anything on both the inside and outside!"[21]

Creating and implementing learning opportunities for middle school students can be challenging, but it is important to remember that they *can* connect with historical content—it just needs to be packaged for them in an appropriate manner. These responses capture how well the students connected with the tour guide and the content. Ranger John used emotional relevance and Douglass's life story to connect with the desire of middle school students to be part of something bigger than themselves.

High School (Ages 13–18)

Older students can entertain more sophisticated discussions about slavery. However, just as with younger students, if they cannot find relevance or an emotional connection, they are likely to shut down. They will also shut down if an adult is condescending or disrespectful to them, or if they perceive they are being treated like a child. High school students are trying to navigate the transition from childhood to adulthood, and they demand respect for their "adult" qualities. Older adolescents are looking to assert themselves, so provide them with activities that allow them to express their opinions or even argue one side of a historical debate.

Students of this age also crave autonomy. Think about developing an activity that allows them to do focused exploration of an object, document, or exhibit and then develop their own opinion or response to it. One option is to give them the freedom to create a dramatic response to a serious topic. At the Moffatt-Ladd House, the staff created a program in collaboration with classroom teachers in which students investigate and respond to an amazing historic document. In a 1779 petition, twenty enslaved men from Portsmouth used the rhetoric of the American Revolution to solicit freedom from the New Hampshire colonial government. After touring the house and learning about the life of Prince Whipple, an enslaved man believed to be the petition's primary author, students work in groups to imagine the genesis of the idea. They discuss what might have influenced the words the enslaved men used in the petition, including how some enslaved people like Prince traveled outside of the city and heard rhetoric of freedom and liberty; the myriad of important Revolutionary-era thinkers coming and going from the house and town; and what an enslaved person's world was like and what they might have heard from the free Black community in Portsmouth.

Then, students coalesce around what they determine to be the most important ideas from their discussion. Staff and teachers give them the freedom to develop a theory as to how the twenty enslaved men initiated the ideas for the petition. Students have responded in a variety of ways, including writing a rap (a la the musical *Hamilton*), a spoken-word piece using the petition as a counterpart of the Black Lives Matter movement; and a fictious dialogue of a conversation between Prince and his enslaver William Whipple. Although the end products are often very powerful, Moffatt-Ladd House director Dr. Barbara McLean Ward noted, "It's not the end-product that matters, it's the dialogue [in the process] that matters. It's about the emotion and the connection they make with the history."[22]

As in the above example, high school students can read and analyze primary sources as part of a tour, although it should not be the majority of the program. One rule of thumb is that activities should not be something they can easily do in a classroom. Think about why they are coming to your site. Use the power of place—your historic structures, landscapes, and objects—to illustrate the stories in the documents. "When students read primary sources . . . with strong authorial voice," Nancy Ogden, Catherine Perkins, and David M. Donahue note, "they are more likely to read like historians . . . bring[ing] together affective responses, understanding derived from conversation with others about text, mental processing, and prior and new knowledge of facts, texts, and the disciplines [to] construct meaning."[23] These sources are actual accounts from the past and become the authoritative voice about slavery. This takes the pressure off staff from being the "experts" about slavery.

Documents like these also help students make deep emotional connections to the content and people from the past.

Multi-Age Groups

It would be simpler for museum educators if all groups came with students in the same grade or age range, but that is not always the case. Mixed-grade schools and multi-age homeschool cooperatives are common. The key is to not always play to the lowest common denominator. Using the aforementioned tips for each age group, it is possible to blend interpretive techniques so that every group member gains something from the experience. This also applies to multi-age family groups.

Homeschool Groups

One way to approach multi-aged groups, like homeschoolers, is to use differentiated instruction—that is, instruction or activities matched to the students' developmental level. Divide the group into two or three small groups of close-age cohorts and give each an age-appropriate version of the same question. When students report out to the larger group, younger students can scaffold their own knowledge by presenting their answers first and then adding information shared by the older students to what they have learned.

Keep in mind that homeschool groups may "not be used to working in a highly structured classroom environment . . . [they might be] less familiar with behavioral expectations like raising hands, following a strict schedule, listening to group instructions, or asking permission," so it's important to collaborate with them to develop clear behavioral expectations at the outset.[24] One of the advantages of working with homeschool groups is that the parents are used to being directly involved with their children's education, so you can put them to work helping you facilitate small groups. Homeschoolers are independent learners, so asking them for their opinion is right in line with their learning style. They are also keen to ask lots of questions to integrate new understandings into their existing knowledge.

Family Groups

Family groups, defined here as a multigenerational group with one or more individuals under the age of eighteen and one or more over the age of eighteen, are an important target audience for most historic sites and museums. According to Colleen Dilenschneider, most of this audience segment visits museums to spend time together. Her research from the IMPACTS National Awareness, Attitudes, and Usage Study of over 98,000 U.S. adults showed that twice as many respondents said the best thing about a visit to a cultural organization was spending time with family and friends.[25] According to Lynn Dierking,

> [Family learning] includes social interaction, collaboration and sharing among members. Through conversations and observations of one another, knowledge and understanding [are] constructed by the family and this learning is incorporated into a family narrative, a

set of shared meanings among and between family members. This interaction, collaboration, and sharing can be direct (a family participating together in an activity or experience) or indirect (a family discussing or doing something together after an experience a child or adult has had elsewhere). . . . Families learn history together best in multi-sensory ways that include engaging in activities . . . and discussing what they are experiencing in relationship to their own everyday lives."[26]

Museum educators can use family dynamics to help foster learning. Family members know each other's capabilities, and often adults can make personal references for the children in their lives that will help the kids make meaning from what they are seeing. One way to do this would be to ask the family groups within your tour or program to turn and talk about a question you pose for them. For example, "Was there ever a time that you weren't allowed to do something that you really wanted to do? What happened? How did that make you feel?" This turn-and-talk technique allows family groups to exchange stories. When you follow this question with the story of an enslaved person, the educator helps the family build understanding about how enslaved people did not have agency to make their own decisions. Yes, a child's experience of not being able to have ice cream for dessert is in no way analogous to the condition of chattel slavery, but it is one way for a child to feel a connection and then explore why it is not the same. Because most younger people understand adults have the freedom to do whatever they want, by asking them to think about the concept of adults not having the freedom to make their own decisions, kids gain perspective on the institution of slavery.

Families are at the mercy of the needs of their most demanding members (of any age). Bathroom breaks, boredom, hunger, distraction—it is all there. Educators and tour guides need to roll with it and consider these needs when building a program or interpretive experience for families. Can families flow in and out of the experience without missing anything? What if they talk over you or ask questions unrelated to the program content? Perhaps you create a packet that they take with them when they leave, allowing them to return to the content at their own pace and address lingering questions and concerns. Working with families often requires more patience than working with school groups, but that does not mean they cannot have a successful learning experience.

The USS Constitution Museum's "Engage Families" study found that families are seeking an authentic experience—"content, materials, environments, and activities."[27] Just like with a well-rounded education program for any age group, ensure your program includes artifacts (reproduction or otherwise), primary source documents, language, and stories that are relevant to your site and its narrative. Share stories about the families, enslaved and free, who lived at your site. It is okay to talk with kids about enslaved families being separated and sold away. You might ask families, "What would you miss most about each other if you had to go away and not see your family for a long time?" Separation was a reality of an enslaved person's experience, and children can relate to the horrifying thought of being parted from their family and may empathize with the traumatic experience.[28] Finally, the reality of separation might be all too real for families, including separation by Immigration and Customs Enforcement, adoption, or the foster care system. Be prepared to honor and respond to these comments when they arise.

Parents Know Best (Sometimes)

Parents often know whether or not they want their children to hear about the realities of slavery, so it is important to be very clear in your marketing, signage, and program introduction that you will be talking about slavery and the lives of enslaved people. Let parents know you will be using age-appropriate language and concepts. Have information available for parents on how to handle the inevitable post-visit questions that children will have either in the car on the way home or in the future when something prompts their memory. Having a pamphlet available onsite or online that includes responses to commonly asked kid questions, discussion prompts, or age-appropriate follow-up reading is key to helping parents continue their child's learning.

You may at some point encounter the parent who knows everything—correctly or incorrectly. Do not shame the adult in front of the child. Just as with adults in groups with other adults, no one wants to lose face. You can gently guide the misinformation toward a new understanding: "Actually, our research shows that enslaved people here . . ." or "We prefer not to think of (insert name of slave owner here) in such binary terms as 'good master' or 'bad master.' People two hundred years ago were just as complicated as we are now, and slavery was a very extreme institution that had very negative implications for all involved." It is important to not perpetuate stereotypes and misconceptions about slavery, but also important not to shame or embarrass a parent in front of their child.

Also be aware how cultural differences in child-rearing and how they learn as a unit affects how families experience your museum or site. Many African American families may have already had conversations about slavery and race, and international families may bring with them their home country's history of slavery or racism. Being sensitive to a family's cultural traditions and habits will make your institution a welcoming place for all.[29]

What Words Should I Use?

With all programs, but especially with students, we must create a common vocabulary. One way to do this is to ask students what a word means, or what they think of when you say a particular word, and then you can come to a common understanding before moving forward. At the beginning of a fourth-grade school program at Historic London Town, the tour guide asked students, "What does it mean to be enslaved?" Students responded with a variety of answers, including "they have to do stuff and don't get paid" and "they work for an owner." Once they reached an understanding of the term "enslaved," the tour guide used only that term during the tour, instead of using the term "slave." It is revealing that students only used the term "slave" in pre-visit surveys, yet in post-visit surveys four of twelve used the term "enslaved." They had absorbed the word and were properly using it in sentences.

We should not dumb down our content for younger students. In this example from Historic Fort Snelling, notice how the staff took the narrative and adapted it for younger visitors. The following is excerpted from their "Cultures in the Kitchen Interpretive Station Treatment."

[INTERPRETER'S NOTE] Though we don't have much primary source information to inform our interpretation of slavery at Fort Snelling, we are able to look at the contemporary historical record from other locations to create informed interpretation of this subject. As interpreters at Historic Fort Snelling, it's important not to shy away from interpreting the history of violence, abuse, and rape of enslaved people. However, the interpretation of violence should be sensitive to the audience and worked in when appropriate. Below are some suggested ways of communicating this content:

[FOR ADULTS] Slavery was a system maintained by physical and psychological violence. Slaveowners sometimes used the threat of violence to maintain power and control, but often they relied on actual physical violence against enslaved people. Sexual violence and the rape of enslaved women was a well-documented and common occurrence throughout the history of slavery in America and here at Fort Snelling. These acts were often committed in locations away from the view of others, including in kitchens.

[FOR CHILDREN] Slaveowners considered enslaved people their property, just like furniture, tools, or even animals. They didn't see them as people like them, and because of this, slaveowners felt it was okay to hurt or abuse enslaved men, women, and children if they didn't do what the slaveowner wanted. Oftentimes, this would happen in places away from where others might see, like the kitchen.

As you can see, the staff is not addressing rape and sexual violence with young audiences, but they are confronting the brutal reality of the institution of slavery. Notice how the institution used age-appropriate language to discuss the horrors of slavery.

At any age, museums and sites must guide students in their learning about slavery by helping them find relevance and make emotional connections to the content. Students need to see why people of the past are important today, and how they, themselves, are empowered toward agency and action in their lives.

Notes

1. Stephen J. Thornton and Ronald Vukelich, "Effects of Children's Understanding of Time Concepts on Historical Understanding," *Theory & Research in Social Education* 16, no.1 (July 2012): 79.
2. Thornton and Vukelich, "Effects of Children's Understanding," 74.
3. Anita Woolfolk, *Educational Psychology* (Boston: Allyn and Bacon, 1980).
4. Chip Wood, *Yardsticks: Child and Adolescent Development Ages 4–14* (Turners Falls, MA: Center for Responsive Schools, 2017).
5. Wood, *Yardsticks*, 55. Adapted from Reich Rawson's list.
6. Anna Forgerson Hindley and Julie Olsen Edwards, "Early Childhood Racial Identity—The Potential Powerful Role for Museum Programing," *Journal of Museum Education* 42, no. 1 (February 2017): 17.

7. Anna Forgerson Hindley, interview with the author, March 23, 2017.

8. Hindley and Edwards, "Early Childhood Racial Identity," 17.

9. Dr. Beverly Tatum, "It's Not So Black and White: Discussing Race and Racism in the Classroom," Scholastic.com, accessed May 29, 2021, https://www.scholastic.com/teachers/articles/teaching-content/its-not-so-black-and-white/.

10. Ellen Levine, Kadir Nelson, and Jerry Dixon, *Henry's Freedom Box* (Solon, OH: Findaway World, 2019).

11. Jonah Winter and Terry Widener, *My Name Is James Madison Hemings* (New York: Schwartz & Wade, 2016).

12. Richard Josey, "Teaching Slavery in Upper Elementary: An Interview with Richard Josey," Thrive in Grade Five, accessed August 19, 2018, http://thriveingradefive.com/teaching-slavery-in-upper-elementary-an-interview-with-scholar-richard-josey/.

13. Tatum, "It's Not So Black and White."

14. Tatum, "It's Not So Black and White."

15. Tatum, "It's Not So Black and White."

16. The museum is on the site of London Town, founded in 1683 as a colonial trading port. The open-air museum consists of one original historic structure, the William Brown House (used as a tavern), a reconstructed Carpenter's Shop and Lord Mayor's Tenement with kitchen garden, ropewalk, and an eighteenth-century tobacco barn. (Historic London Town, accessed February 16, 2018, https://www.historiclondontown.org/history.)

17. "Aiken-Rhett House Scavenger Hunt—Upper Elementary School," Historic Charleston Foundation, 2015.

18. "The Adolescent Brain—Learning Strategies and Teaching Tips," n.d.; accessed June 16, 2018, http://spots.wustl.edu/SPOTS%20manual%20Final/SPOTS%20Manual%204%20Learning%20Strategies.pdf.

19. "The Adolescent Brain."

20. "The Adolescent Brain."

21. Student feedback from post-visit surveys at Frederick Douglass National Historic Site, March 30, 2017.

22. Dr. Barbara McLean Ward, interview with the author, April 16, 2018.

23. Nancy Ogden, Catherine Perkins, and David M. Donahue, "Not a Peculiar Institution: Challenging Students' Assumptions about Slavery in U.S. History," *Society for History Education* 41, no. 4 (August 2008): 472.

24. "Beyond Programs: Other Ways to Work with Schools," Nova Scotia Museum, accessed July 14, 2018. https://museum.novascotia.ca/sites/default/files/inline/documents/toolbox2016/nsm_toolbox_-_module_seven_2016.pdf.

25. Colleen Dilenschneider, "The Value of Shared Learning Experiences within Cultural Organizations," *Know Your Own Bone*, accessed July 14, 2018, https://www.colleendilen.com/2016/07/13/the-value-of-shared-experiences-within-cultural-organizations-data/.

26. Lynn Dierking, "What Is Family Learning," *Engage Families*, accessed July 14, 2018. https://engagefamilies.org/family-learning-101/what-is-family-learning/.

27. "Authentic and Distinctive," *Engage Families*, accessed July 14, 2018, https://engagefamilies.org/design/authentic-and-distinctive/.

28. For additional information on techniques for creating inclusive family learning experiences, visit http://engagedfamilies.org.

29. For additional information on training staff to work with families, visit the Boston Children's Museum "Learning Together" guide, http://www.bostonchildrensmuseum.org/exhibits -programs/museum-professionals/learning-together-museum-staff-training-curriculum.

Fostering Empathy

"Cultivate a sense of empathy . . . put yourself in other people's shoes . . . see the world from their eyes. Empathy is a quality of character that can change the world—one that makes you understand that your obligations to others extend beyond people who look like you and act like you and live in your neighborhood."[1] —Barack Obama

WHEN BUILDING programs for an audience of children and teens, whether school or family groups, it is absolutely vital to give careful consideration to the interpretive techniques and methodologies you will use. This and the subsequent two chapters cover a variety of interpretive techniques. Chapter 5 addresses specific techniques I have found to be successful in helping students build empathy with historical actors. Chapters 6 and 7 address techniques for building engagement and dialogue. Although I have categorized these techniques into particular chapters, many of them could just as well fit into one of the other two chapters, as empathy, engagement, and dialogue are not mutually exclusive. However, I have organized them this way to highlight why I believe certain techniques work better than others to convey content or accomplish a certain goal.

What Is Empathy and Why Does It Matter?

Empathy is currently receiving a lot of airtime in museum circles. Research, articles, books, and conference presentations are focusing on how museums can play a significant role in helping build a more empathic society.[2] In general, helping children develop empathy is important because it helps them build a sense of security and stronger relationships with their peers and adults, and encourages tolerance and acceptance of others.[3] "Empathy is a work in progress throughout childhood and adolescence. While we are born hardwired with the capacity for empathy, its development requires experience and practice."[4] As we age, we gain emotional and cognitive understandings of empathy while "testing" out its uses in the world around us. When a young person has developed empathy, that person

- understands that she is a distinct person from those around her and that other people may have different feelings and perspectives than her own.
- can recognize feelings in herself and others and name them.
- can regulate her own emotional responses.
- can put herself in someone else's shoes and imagine how someone might feel.
- can imagine what kind of action or response might help a person feel better.[5]

This connects back to my points in chapter 2—what is a "successful" program at your site, what is the goal of your program, and why should people care that you are developing programs on the history and legacies of slavery. Helping students build social-emotional skills while learning history and making relevant connections to their lives today is a win-win-win.

Simply put, empathy is about emotional connection. Social psychologist Brené Brown notes, "Empathy fuels connection. . . . [E]mpathy is a vulnerable choice, because in order to connect with you, I have to connect with something within myself that knows that feeling. [I have to] recogniz[e] their perspective as their truth."[6] It is an affective state in which the learner acknowledges feelings that another person could be expected to have, based on a degree of understanding of that other person's emotional situation.

Conversely, a learner experiencing sympathy feels their own feelings of sadness or compassion in response to the other's situation.[7] In planning interpretive experiences, it is helpful to distinguish between the goal of helping learners better understand the experiences of and relate to historical actors through empathy, and the goal of encouraging learners to feel compassion for historical actors through sympathy. We want students to connect on an emotional level, to empathize with the emotions of family separation by connecting it to a time in their lives when they were separated from someone they loved, rather than feeling sorry for a separated family they do not know. While connecting empathically to enslaved people is difficult, it is also essential as an exercise in developing empathy for people whose freedom, choice, and the ability to unreservedly use their own voices was curtailed through violence. Young learners gain valuable lessons of empathy and empowerment as they study the lives of others, past and present.

It is important to cultivate empathy when interpreting slavery with children and teens because understanding the emotional and psychological impact of the institution of slavery on the enslaved enhances the learner's understanding of these historical events, their meaning, and their lasting significance. Another reason to foster empathy is to bring to the fore the traditionally marginalized voices of the enslaved and those who lived with the threat of enslavement. Without a conscious attempt to encourage empathy for the enslaved, the study of slavery can easily focus attention on the perspective of those who engaged in and benefited from slavery. Students may learn the mechanisms of slavery but fail to appreciate the impact of the institution on the people most affected by it, the enslaved themselves. They may more easily relate to those who were free than to those who were enslaved, and perhaps only view the latter through the lens of the free.

A final reason for making empathy a deliberate part of the interpretation of slavery is to aid students in their moral and psychological development. Learning to empathize with others, especially those in circumstances fundamentally different from our own, is critical to moral and psychological development. Empathy is indispensable to learning to see diverse peoples as "us" rather than "other." Even though humanizing the other does not actually reverse prejudice, research shows learning about the lives of others can, at least, reduce bias.[8] Students have been gradually cultivating the ability to empathize with others since infancy, but historical study offers a unique opportunity to cultivate and enlarge this skill in more challenging settings than most young people are likely to encounter anywhere else.

Teaching about empathy is a complex process. As we teach, we need to be sure not to take away an enslaved person's agency. In our interpretations, we often assign historical figures emotions and feelings, which we do not know if they experienced, because we imagine that is what they would have experienced. We must balance empathy for someone else without centering our emotions and feelings. We walk a fine line as we place our modern feelings on historical people and events.[9]

Emotions often become entangled with the more intellectual aspects of history, especially when it comes to matters of identity. Encouraging empathy for historical figures, such as those who experienced enslavement, may require offering students new historical narratives and helping them navigate emotions generated by conflicts between these new ideas and ones that students hold in the core of their identities.

To create that balance it is essential that students have a comprehensive narrative of slavery. If students "treat people in the past as less than fully human and do not respond to those people's hopes and fears," Mariruth Leftwich and Amanda McAllen warn, "they have hardly begun to understand what history is about."[10] We must change our mindset for how we tell the stories by finding what Leftwich and McAllen call "common personality attributes that span time, civic issues, and personal experiences that students [can] connect with and identify as being relevant in their own lives."[11]

Empathy has the potential to generate psychological distress in audiences, especially with highly traumatic historical narratives such as slavery. (See chapter 1 for more information on historical trauma.) This distress may or may not involve some of the same emotional responses as the original historical figures had. For example, when we put emphasis on the rape of enslaved women, do we consider the lived experiences of our audience? Who among them may be survivors of sexual assault? Do we take into consideration the triggering effect of our stories of whippings and beatings on audience members who survived abuse or torture? You might consider alerting your visitors to the content of the program prior to starting and provide space—literal and metaphorical—for those who need to process feelings they choose not to share with others.

There are essentially two mechanisms through which psychological distress may arise. In the first case, the historical pain and suffering being conveyed may lie far outside a learner's personal experience, and thus may be shocking and stressful to reckon with. In the second case, a learner may experience psychological distress precisely because they *can* relate to the traumatic events and emotions being relayed. In common parlance, the learner is being *triggered* by being forced to relive, in some way, a traumatic experience from the past.

It is possible to minimize the risk of causing psychological distress when fostering empathy in learners. This chapter discusses specific techniques in various pedagogical contexts. But in general, researchers advise focusing on fostering *empathetic concern* from an outside perspective, rather than encouraging learners to try to make the painful emotional experiences of others their own. As Northwestern University psychologist Adam Waytz says, "When people think about others from a third-person perspective, they experience empathy, empathic concern, and they want to help people. And that's the goal. Where people actually take on the pain of another person, that doesn't lead to helping, it leads to disengagement, it's this 'ouch' experience."[12] The goals of fostering empathy should involve encouraging emotional development in the learner, in addition to developing an understanding of historical persons.[13]

Before discussing approaches to fostering empathy, it is worth noting that not all aspects of the institution of slavery should have empathy as a goal. We never want to put students in the position of taking on the role of advocating for slavery. For example, we can share with students why a slave trader might have made the choices he did and how economic motives shaped the details of the trade without necessarily encouraging students to *empathize* with a slave trader. Younger students need not appreciate the emotional state of slave traders or slave masters to humanize them or to comprehend their motives or justifications for their actions. Chapter 6 discusses role-playing in more detail, but in short, there is no good reason for a seven-, ten-, or even thirteen-year-old to impersonate a slave holder's opinion on slavery, as we do not want them to have to argue for the inherent evil they are being told to represent. Students can just as easily learn about a slave holder or slave trader's perspective on this issue by reading first-person accounts—but not acting them out or empathizing with an enslaver's actions.

As we shift perspectives on the Founding Fathers to include their role as enslavers, it is important that high school students consider Washington, Jefferson, and others in light of their motivations—the conflicting emotions, economic incentives, and desire for power that led these men to not only become but to continue to be enslavers. If we ask young people to reevaluate the words of the founding documents, we must also ask them to sit with the questions of why these men (and women) enslaved fellow humans, what motivated them, what caused them to act this way, and what led them to make these decisions? We must ask learners to consider Jefferson in light of the glaring hypocrisy between his words and actions, and the utter emotional conflict he wrestled with while trying to maintain his position in society, while at the same time addressing him as someone who actively bought, sold, had sexual relations with, and fathered children with, those he enslaved.[14]

At the very least, learning about the daily lives, personal relationships, and accomplishments of the enslaved, rather than simply those of free people of European descent, can foster a respect and understanding that the enslaved have so often been denied. Remember that no matter how much our interpretation humanizes or empathizes with enslaved people, slavery trapped them in a terrorizing institution that stole their humanity, freedom, and families. Enslaved people were constantly looked upon as less than people of European descent. This is the point a tour at Poplar Forest overlooked. The historic site's otherwise enlightening *Enslaved Community Tour* included stories of those Jefferson enslaved, their trials (being beaten by an overseer or sold by Jefferson) and agency (being paid by Jefferson for extra work), but the tour guide neglected two major points. He never mentioned the enslaved community was made up of African or African-descended people, missing an opportunity to connect race and slavery. While it is logical to assume visitors already knew this fact, it was unwise to do so, given how essential race is to the history of slavery. As he waxed on about how privileged the enslaved community at Poplar Forest was—Jefferson recognized their marriages and gave them gifts when they wed—he never underscored the liberty-robbing institution to which they were bound. The tour guide missed the opportunity to explain why people of African descent were at Poplar Forest in the first place and that race and bondage were the basic elements of slavery as an institution in southern life. Marriage between enslaved people was a way for enslavers to establish family bonds that could be weaponized in an effort to control enslaved people's actions. Addressing Jefferson's approval of marriage as a gift made him seem a benevolent enslaver, rather than the perpetrator of ongoing psychological abuse, leaving visitors with an incomplete picture of the lives of those Jefferson enslaved.

Fostering Empathy through Shared Experiences

Humans also develop empathy through shared experiences. Through these experiences, we can develop the capacity for empathy and the ability to draw connections between ourselves and others. The shared experience must impart knowledge—in part because fostering empathy is never the only goal of interpretation, and in part because students cannot get a sense of others' feelings without knowing something of their circumstances. An effective experience is also likely to engage the senses and to be immersive, to one degree or another, qualities that serve to enhance the development of empathy, in contrast to mere intellectual engagement. For example, visitors to Cape Coast Castle in Ghana have a very immersive, emotional, and spiritual experience when they tour the fort's dungeon where enslavers incarcerated captive Africans prior to forcing them aboard ships to the Western Hemisphere. Being inside the dark, poorly ventilated stone walls and high vaulted ceilings creates a chilling connection to those wrenched from their families and forced into captivity. The power of place—the damp interior of a slave dungeon, the middle of a vast cotton field, or the rough-hewn walls of a cabin—provides an immersive connection to the past. To be effective at generating empathy organically, an experience must shift the learner's perspective so that they are fully engaged, rather than merely asking the learner to passively absorb sensory data.

Fostering Empathy through Primary Sources

Another empathy-fostering technique is using primary sources. Using simple prompts and a narrative, museum educators can help students engage their imaginations without having to role-play an enslaved person. Andrea Jones, founder of Peak Experience Lab told us about one Middle Passage visualization activity she used as a middle school teacher. Her first rule for any type of activity like this is to allow students to opt in or opt out of the activity, and they can opt out at any time once it begins. This is key because it gives students agency and control over their own social-emotional well-being.

To set up the activity, Jones explained to her students that they would not play the role of an enslaved person or simulate the Middle Passage experience and she, the teacher, wasn't playing a slave master or ship's captain. Jones clearly articulated that they were *not* pretending to be enslaved—an important point to underscore multiple times so that students understand the scope and gravitas of the activity. She was being herself—the teacher/facilitator that the students knew and trusted. Next, Jones had students lie down on the floor, close together but not touching. She played faint sounds of ocean waves and turned off the lights. From that position, she had each student read a quote from Olaudah Equiano's *Interesting Narrative of the Life of Olaudah Equiano*, the memoir of his experience of the Middle Passage. Jones recalled students found powerful the simple act of intently listening to each other's voices but not being able to see who was speaking.

At the end of the activity, Jones read a passage about the concept of an enslaved person being considered property from Julius Lester's *To Be a Slave.* In conclusion, she asked students how they think the legacies of slavery affect their relationships today. She shared that it was important for her to be vulnerable as the facilitator of the activity. Being open and honest with students throughout gave them permission to share deeper feelings during the post-activity dialogue.

Fostering Empathy through Storytelling

Stories are a natural vehicle for promoting empathy with others and humans have been communicating through and learning from them for millennia. Sharing stories is a social action and we are social beings. Museums provide the sort of personal details and narratives routinely offered in storytelling and social discourse. We should use the social interaction of storytelling in museums to promote empathy with real historical figures with whom we can never interact. Good storytelling provides interesting information and a narrative arc that engages the listener in anticipation of how the story will unfold.

Of course, there are limits to how well we can mimic direct social engagement with historical figures. Being social creatures, we respond best to face-to-face contact, in which we can see and hear directly from the storyteller and can offer social cues in response (facial expressions, encouraging words and sounds, even questions as prompts). To mimic these aspects of social interaction, we naturally seek to use the words of the historic figures themselves. Whether via exhibit text, audio or video recordings, dramatic readings, first-person interpretation, or museum theater, stories are our stock-in-trade—they are how we do business.

During a visit to George Washington's Mount Vernon, I observed a very simple and effective storytelling technique that captured the imagination of students and honored the lives of those enslaved by the Washingtons. At the end of the tour, the high school students gathered at the Slave Memorial, the final resting place for members of Mount Vernon's enslaved community. As students assembled around the memorial, the tour guide explained what is known about the burial ground and those interred there. She then asked for four students to read aloud short biographies of people enslaved at Mount Vernon who may be buried in the hallowed ground beneath their feet. The brief biographical stories captured what little is known about these people's lives, but paints a vivid picture of a living, breathing person.

It is my pleasure to celebrate the life of Barbara. Barbara lived at Mansion House Farm. She was the daughter of Kitty, a dairy maid, and Isaac, the head carpenter. Barbara was the second youngest in a family of eight girls. Barbara may have carried large pails of water around the estate, gathered sticks for firewood, and cared for her younger sister while her parents worked. She was 10 in 1799, the year that George Washington died. Barbara's father was freed through Washington's will, but the rest of the family were dower slaves and were not freed.

Today we remember Barbara.[15]

These simple sentences, information pulled directly from documents her enslavers wrote, captured Barbara's life and made her life more relatable to the students gathered. It stated the names and occupations of her parents, her place in the birth order, how many siblings she had, her job responsibilities, and noted what happened to her at the tender age of ten upon Washington's death. The four biographies—two males and two females, all children or teens—gave students an immediate connection point with the past. The guide did not ask students to play a role, only to give voice to the precious few details that have survived of the life of an enslaved person at Mount Vernon.

It was a powerful moment to witness. The solemnity with which the high school students treated the moment was remarkable. They approached the activity with an air of respect and compassion, one the students carried with them afterward. For example, in a post-visit survey about the impact of this activity, a student remarked, "When we were at the enslaved people's grave and we took the moment of silence, I felt like they were there, and they were happy that things have changed, and I felt like crying because they were basically just put in the ground because that's where they put the dead bodies."[16] This feeling of sad peace was beyond an empathetic experience, crossing into a spiritual one.[17]

Fostering Empathy through Museum Theater

During the commemoration of the abolition of Britain's Atlantic slave trade, the International Slavery Museum in Liverpool offered an engaging piece of museum theater that brought to life the story of American slavery for student visitors. The museum framed the school program as "an immersive experiential interaction . . . that dramatizes a past that is beyond living memory."[18]

An actor portrayed Ellen Craft, a light-skinned enslaved woman who disguised herself as a man and escaped north from Georgia in 1850 with her enslaved husband William masquerading as her enslaved servant. Following a script, the actress recounted their lives enslaved on a southern plantation, her father as her owner, and the harrowing escape she and William made to freedom. The students also learned how the Crafts became abolitionists, traveling the world to share their story, and making their way to London where they settled to raise a family. At the end of her performance, during which the students sat with rapt attention, "Ellen Craft" took questions from the audience, facilitated by a staff educator. Post-visit surveys of the students helped gauge the experience and the efficacy of the interpretive methodology. Evaluations reported that the performance and question session made quite an impression on the students.

When comparing the students' pre- and post-visit responses, evaluations showed students reflected on their learning experience at the museum and the significance of the institution of slavery. One student's "generic" response to a pre-visit question about why it was important to learn about slavery stands in stark contrast to the reflective response to the same post-visit question.

- Pre-visit: "Without an event like that our world and ourselves would possibly not be in the format [that] it is today."
- Post-visit: "[It] tells us what cruel and un-dignified things that were forced upon people just because of their skin color in that because we are white we have control over everything and try to act like god."[19]

Museum theater has the power to create transformative empathetic experiences for students.

Hiring actors to portray historical people in museum theater is an important, but sometimes costly, feature of this methodology. Professional actors will follow the well-researched scripts you provide them and do the additional research they need to develop their characters to embody a story in movements, facial expressions, and vocal patterns. Museum staff members with acting talent may also take on this challenge; however, there is a big difference between someone who acts and someone who reenacts. Professionally trained actors know how to create a character and give it life on stage. Most reenactors lack professional training in character development and, in my experience, are more about creating the ambiance of the situation (clothing and kit) than in portraying a multi-dimensional person. Another critical difference is that actors are trained to perform for an audience—again this idea of a learner-centered experience—versus reenactors who tend to be in the experience for their own enjoyment. Knowing this difference and responding accordingly is critical for the visitor experience.

Fostering Empathy through First-Person Interpretation

It was at Mount Vernon that I saw the effectiveness of actor-interpreters firsthand, when two African American actors portrayed people enslaved by the Washingtons as part of a program for high school students. During a tour of the Mansion House Farm, the tour guide led the group into the stable yard. At this point the students were about thirty minutes into the tour, and although they seemed interested, they were not all that engaged. This group of mostly Black and Latinx students had been attentive to the white tour guide, but when the two African American actors showed up the students' energy changed.

Caroline Branham, portrayed by Brenda Parker, appeared first in search of her son Peter. Caroline Branham was enslaved by Martha Washington, known as a "dower slave" because Branham was part of Martha's inheritance upon her first husband's death. Branham was an enslaved housemaid and seamstress for the Washingtons. Parker launched into an emotionally compelling interpretation, talking about how many of the people enslaved at Mount Vernon lived in constant fear that their families would be separated. She explained, in heart-wrenching language, how she was a dower slave and that when Washington dies his will only emancipates the people he owns; therefore, she will not be free. The students were hanging on her every word.

She was then interrupted by Christopher Sheels, portrayed by Jonathon Woods. Christopher Sheels served Washington as his enslaved valet and personal manservant. Woods immediately connected with the students—explaining that one of his tasks was to shave Washington and it appeared as if some of the men in our group did a good job shaving themselves. There was tentative laughter among the group, almost a bit of relief after the intensity of Caroline Branham's story. Woods, as Sheels, went on to beautifully articulate that "the General was of two minds": he fought for freedom, yet he owned slaves, quoting Washington's contradictory writings about slavery. "This is the man I contend with," Woods said. "He secured my life when I got sick but sold my wife from me. Both sides are right that hold Washington as hero and slave owner."

Then a student asked, "Where's your wife?"

Woods paused, looked down, and an expression of grief crossed his face. The students perceptibly leaned in toward him. It was a beautiful moment—the students were with him *in* the story. In character, he explained what happened to Sheels and his wife. He finished by saying, "Freedom is not free. I think about it all the time." The students burst into applause. As the students were leaving the stable yard and following the tour guide to the next stop, one young woman said, "It got me when he froze after she asked about his wife."[20] A male classmate agreed with her.

The students' responses in the post-visit survey continued to illuminate the success of this interpretive technique.

- "The impression Caroline gave about their lack of freedom to marry made me so sad to think the things I feel everyone has the right to they were deprived. Even something as important as family."
- "When a student asked Christopher about his wife. I was very emotional from the way he looked. He showed such grief that it made me feel it."
- "Christopher Sheels spoke of George Washington as a man of two minds. The appreciation he held for Washington's more sympathetic side was evident, although he detested his slave-holding as a value. His deeply-rooted emotions over his enslaved loved ones, including himself, were exposed through his touching performance."[21]

Thanks to the brilliant and affective first-person interpretation skills of Parker and Woods, the students made strong empathetic connections to the lives of Caroline Branham and Christopher Sheels.

After the tour, Woods and Parker each shared with me how they developed the characters of Christopher Sheels and Caroline Branham, and what it is like to portray them daily. Woods describes his work as

being affective with the information and the stark reality of slavery. Telling the story truthfully, with integrity and dignity, but with grace. Balancing the humanity of the enslaved people without vilifying George Washington. Taking students' realities and clashing them against slavery. I always bring it back to Washington—making connections between the injustices of slavery and his participation in it.[22]

In a post-tour conversation with the students, the actors also touched on the difficulties of being an African American person portraying an eighteenth-century enslaved person and interacting with visitors. When asked about the different types of reactions she gets from guests, Parker teared up: "I've had people pull away because they know what I represent. If I don't speak for the ancestors, who will?"[23] Woods added, "There are some days I don't want to talk about slavery. It weighs on you. As a man of color, there are many levels of inequity that I deal with that I bring to the character's mannerisms."[24]

It's not easy for Black or white people to portray the history of slavery in first person. The emotional weight of the content manifests not just in interpretive interactions with visitors, but also in one's personal life. If someone is going to portray an enslaved person or an enslaver, they need to be prepared for the constant blurring of past and present. Shannon Little, a former staff member of the Accokeek Foundation, an organization that educates people about the natural and cultural heritage of Piscataway Park, Maryland, including an eighteenth-century tobacco plantation, explained why she left a job portraying an enslaved person:

> If you think that you're interpreting the past, it's implied that it's something that's far removed and maybe something that's actually healed. But, with all the recent events [police brutality against Black people, the Charleston church shooting] in the country that have been in the spotlight . . . the past and the present start to blend. . . . I was questioning why I was doing it [portraying an enslaved person] because after all that my ancestors did have to go through, why would I want to relive this type of trauma? Especially since we're not far removed from those politics and ideologies. It felt weird interpreting something that was supposed to be the past, but really isn't the past.[25]

It's also important to remember that interpreting history in first person should not just be a one-way medium. From its origin in the early twentieth century to its growing popularity mid-century, first-person interpretation has been primarily a passive experience for visitors. If we want our students to engage with the historical content, they must be physically, emotionally, and mentally engaged with the historical characters, as evidenced by the students' connection with and response to Woods/Sheels and Parker/Branham at Mount Vernon.

Fostering Empathy though Exhibit-Engagement Techniques

Encouraging students to empathize with a historical person does not have to involve either actors in a stable yard or students reading a biography in a cemetery, as in the examples provided above. A student activity at Ford's Theatre in Washington, DC, revealed that a simple unfacilitated exhibit technique could elicit the empathetic connection educators were looking for. Ford's Theatre, a site of political violence, encapsulates many contradictory topics, including slavery and emancipation, treason and revenge, and celebration and death—all challenging topics to interpret. In 2018, staff of the Ford's Theatre Society were rapidly prototyping low-cost, short-term solutions for engaging students in an outdated and static exhibit in the theater's basement. The staff chose four historical figures—Elizabeth Keckley, William Henry Seward, James Tanner, and Julia Taft—to represent what they called a "balance of male and female, different ages, different races, and a mix of well-known and 'regular' people."[26] To help students empathize with a person who was part of Lincoln's world, staff handed students a card featuring one of these people. Students were directed to look for flip labels that corresponded with the name on the card to reveal the person's connection to different episodes in the Lincoln assassination. The first corresponding label asked a question meant to engender empathy. For example, to help students appreciate the significance of Fanny Stewart's meeting with famous actor, and assassin's brother, Edwin Booth, the label asks, "Have you ever met a famous person? How did you react?" Other questions include, "Do you have a skill that might be useful in an emergency?," "What would you do if you knew people who were doing terrible things?," and "What would you do for freedom?"[27]

During their formative evaluation phase, the Ford's Theatre staff conducted post-visit interviews and found the cards helped the students connect with the past.

- "Teachers and students reported the cards gave them something on which to actively focus attention and helped frame their paths [in the exhibit] and gave shape to the visit. Staff observations backed this up."
- "Students took ownership of their assigned characters and expressed feeling invested in that person. They were less likely to follow the path of characters that were not 'theirs,' though some took multiple pathways."
- "Students felt it was critical that the cards represent real people, not composite historical figures. They liked Julia Taft, saying she was the most relatable because she was their age. We also had multiple requests for cards representing the Lincoln boys."
- "Students liked having 'everyday' people on the cards, noting we should have only a few famous ones."[28]

In a final round of prototyping, Ford's staff found students related better to younger characters and engaged more with female characters. They were particularly, the report notes, "intrigued by Anna Surratt's relationship with the conspirators and advised us to keep her as a character."[29] At the time of this writing, staff were still working on the activity's conclusion, as currently students follow their character's journey through the exhibit and return the card to a bin at the end of the exhibit. The staff tried to get students to vote whether they liked or disliked the activity and on their empathy for their character.[30] However, they were concerned the term "vote" seemed too trivial for the content of the exhibit, and students did not see the connection to the activity. Whatever way they choose to end the activity, this simple, inexpensive prototype helped staff develop a successful activity through which students could connect to and empathize with people from the past.

Fostering Empathy through Shared Characteristics

In order to reengage their student visitors, the staff of the Senator John Heinz History Center in Pittsburgh sought a new way to connect ninth-grade students with the narrative in their *From Slavery to Freedom* exhibit, which covered the gamut of slavery's history and legacy: from West African culture to the Transatlantic slave trade; to abolition, the Underground Railroad, the Civil War, and Reconstruction; and ultimately to the modern Civil

Rights Movement.[31] Staff learned that students, a majority of whom were African American, found the exhibit's content challenging. They expressed feelings of sadness and anger after visiting it."[32]

In response, staff reframed the self-guided visit to help students better relate to the personal stories in the exhibit. Specifically, a focus on African Americans as change agents, they hoped would replace anger with feelings of empowerment and agency. The staff created an experience that shifted students' mindsets by having them focus on positive characteristics like bravery, curiosity, problem solving, passion, and empathy, which provided them with the opportunity to view these characteristics in historical figures and themselves. Instead of staff-led tours of the exhibit that did not hold their attention, students now explore the space in small groups at their own pace through an activity that encourages them to make connections between objects and images in the exhibit and words like "adversity," "determination," and "freedom." The Heinz History Center's Mariruth Leftwich and Amanda McAllen reported that staff saw positive changes in the students' experience; they "overheard students helping each other to understand the content, adding information that they had learned elsewhere to expand the group's knowledge, and working together to come to terms with the representations of the journey from slavery to freedom depicted in the exhibit."[33] Post-visit feedback showed that almost half of students "made an explicit connection to one of the change-agent mindset characteristics." As one student remarked, "I enjoy learning more about slavery even if it's sad because I'm African American and want to [know] more about my ancestors' lives."[34]

This activity by the Heinz History Center is an example of how the interpretation of slavery within museums and history organizations drives a shift in mindset from enslaved people being powerless and degraded to being agents of change and robust emotional human beings. We can help students see positive connotations to their people's history and help them make empowering connections with their lives today. That is among the greatest interpretive gifts we can give audiences, especially students.

Debriefing the Experience

No matter the activity, a debrief or reflection is a necessary part of any school program. This is particularly true when the goal is to foster empathy. A culminating discussion allows students time to reflect on what they learned, as they may have misunderstandings or questions about the experience. Some students need time to discuss their feelings about the institution of slavery and those who were enslaved, while others need time to process before they can discuss. It is also possible to pose questions for them to address later, so students have more time to think and process. This involves creating robust post-visit materials and helping classroom teachers acquire the necessary skills to lead such dialogues. As Thomas Rockwell and others note, a reflection discussion designed to

> encourage self-disclosure and compassionate listening could be a strong tool to foster prosocial aspects of empathy. That said, merely having a conversation doesn't ensure an empathetic experience. Conversations can confirm stereotypes and even increase other

barriers to empathy. Therefore, it is vital that [programs] prompt empathetic listening and support norms that inspire inclusive and open-minded dialogue.[35]

A reflection gives space for codifying learning and for meaning-making. This is when a-ha moments occur.[36] (See chapter 7 for tips on dialogue techniques.)

Whether through storytelling, first-person interpretation, or museum theater, fostering empathy is an important technique for connecting students with people held in slavery and to how the country has been affected and impacted by its legacies. We must share the stories of the enslaved so that students can better understand the impact of slavery on our world today. By exercising empathy within the study of a complicated subject like slavery, students hone the perspective-taking skills that are so valuable to forming social support networks and building a society in which they understand how other people feel and what they might need. These empathic skills are foundational to achieving a more just and equitable society, and one in which we can start to heal from four hundred years of the enslavement and oppression of fellow human beings.

Notes

1. Barack Obama (University of Massachusetts at Boston Commencement Address, Boston, MA, June 2, 2006).
2. See also *Designing for Empathy: Perspectives on the Museum Experience*, Elif M. Gökçiğdem (Lanham, MD: Rowman & Littlefield, 2019); *Fostering Empathy through Museums*, Elif M. Gökçiğdem (Lanham, MD: Rowman & Littlefield, 2016); and *The Empathic Museum* (http://empatheticmuseum.weebly.com/).
3. "Why Teaching Children Empathy Is More Important than Ever," Good Start Early Learning, accessed January 30, 2021, https://www.goodstart.org.au/news-and-advice/february-2018/why-teaching-children-empathy-is-important#:~:text=Helping%20young%20children%20to%20develop,It%20promotes%20good%20mental%20health.
4. Erin Walsh and David Walsh, "How Children Develop Empathy," *Psychology Today*, May 9, 2019; accessed November 15, 2020, https://www.psychologytoday.com/us/blog/smart-parenting-smarter-kids/201905/how-children-develop-empathy.
5. Ibid.
6. Brene Brown, "The Power of Vulnerability," accessed June 13, 2021, https://www.youtube.com/watch?v=sXSjc-pbXk4.
7. Nancy Eisenberg, Tracy Spinrad, and Adrienne Sadovsky, "Empathy-Related Responding in Children," in *Handbook of Moral Development*, eds. Melanie Killen and Judith G. Smetana (New York: Psychology Press, 2010), 184.
8. Dan R. Johnson, Brandie L. Huffman, and Danny M. Jasper, "Changing Race Boundary Perception by Reading Narrative Fiction," *Basic and Applied Social Psychology* 36, no. 1 (February 2014): 83–90.
9. Nicole Moore, note to the author, September 13, 2020.
10. Mariruth Leftwich and Amanda McAllen, "Be the Change: A Mindset for Museum Teaching," *Journal of Museum Education* 43, no. 4 (October 2018): 395.
11. Ibid.

12. Adam Waytz quoted in "The Limits of Empathy," *Topic*, accessed February 22, 2019, https://www.topic.com/the-limits-of-empathy.

13. Sara D. Hodges and Michael W. Myers, "Empathy," in *Encyclopedia of Social Psychology*, eds. Roy F. Baumeister and Kathleen D. Vohs (Los Angeles: Sage Publications, 2007), 297.

14. Nicole Moore, note to the author, September 13, 2020.

15. Courtesy of Linda Powell, Mount Vernon Ladies Association, email to the author, February 26, 2018.

16. Post-visit survey #3, Mount Vernon, March 23, 2017.

17. A spiritual experience is a reality surpassing normal human understanding. In this case, it was a moment of contemplative prayer in which one has an intuitive encounter with the ancestors.

18. Nikki Spalding, "Learning to Remember and Imagine Slavery: The Pedagogies of Museum Field Trips in the Representation of 'Difficult Histories,'" in *Slavery, Memory, and Identity: National Representations and Global Legacies*," eds. Douglas Hamilton et al. (London: Pickering & Chatto, 2012), 141.

19. Spalding, "Learning to Remember," 145.

20. "Telling Their Stories" tour, Mount Vernon, March 23, 2017.

21. Post-visit surveys 4, 9, and 10, Mount Vernon, March 23, 2017.

22. Jonathan Woods, interview with the author, March 23, 2017.

23. Brenda Parker, interview with the author, March 23, 2017.

24. Jonathan Woods, interview with the author, March 23, 2017.

25. Peak Experiences Lab, accessed March 8, 2018, http://www.peakexperiencelab.com/blog/2017/1/15/5rn1yxf1g74muws51mx3bmek0yupz7.

26. David McKenzie and Kate Haley Goldman, "Prototyping Historical Figure Cards at Ford's Theatre: Sprint 2, Round 2," Ford's Theatre Society, accessed August 19, 2018, https://www.fords.org/blog/post/prototyping-historical-figure-cards-at-fords-theatre-sprint-2-round-2/.

27. David McKenzie, email to the author, May 31, 2019.

28. David McKenzie, email to the author, May 31, 2019.

29. David McKenzie and Kate Haley Goldman, "Following a Historical Figure, Again: Prototyping Sprint 3," Ford's Theatre Society, accessed January 18, 2019, https://www.fords.org/blog/post/following-a-historical-figure-again-prototyping-sprint-3/.

30. McKenzie and Goldman, "Following a Historical Figure, Again."

31. Leftwich and McAllen, "Be the Change," 396.

32. Leftwich and McAllen, "Be the Change," 396.

33. Leftwich and McAllen, "Be the Change," 397.

34. Leftwich and McAllen, "Be the Change," 398.

35. Thomas Rockwell, Heike Winterheld, Joshua Gutwill, and Shawn Lani, "Social Inquiry Exhibits: Fostering Social Learning in Museums," in *Designing for Empathy: Perspectives on the Museum Experience*, ed. Elif M. Gökçiğdem (Lanham, MD: Rowman & Littlefield, 2019), 156.

36. Andrea Jones, interview with the author, March 2, 2018.

CHAPTER 6

Engagement Techniques

"How do you teach events that defy knowledge, experiences that go beyond imagination? How do you tell children, big and small, that society could lose its mind and start murdering its own soul and its own future? How do you unveil horrors without offering at the same time some measure of hope?" —Holocaust survivor Elie Wiesel[1]

HERE ARE some common sentiments expressed by, and observed at, historic sites and museums about engagement techniques they employ in their education programs:

"We do hands-on learning."—Educator passes around an object that students can touch.

"We do active learning."—Students do a scavenger hunt in an exhibit.

"Our programs are interactive."—Students sit in chairs as they watch a PowerPoint and are asked yes/no questions.

These are far from the best ways to engage students with the history of slavery. To paraphrase Wiesel from the quote above, how do we tell children the story about a society that enslaved and murdered fellow human beings? How do we engage students with the horrors of our country's past while offering some measure of hope for our future? Museums must engage students with stories of slavery, but what exactly is engagement and how do we do it? Before getting to the latter, let us first examine the definition of engagement and the educational theory behind the concept. As museum professional Ed Rodley defines it, engagement "is an active, emotional process, one of being attracted and held by something of interest."[2] In the context of this chapter, engagement is the process of connecting young visitors with the stories of enslaved people and the institution of slavery.

Learning is an inherently active pursuit, and it occurs best when our minds, our emotions, *and* our bodies are engaged in it. In the public history world, museum educators often describe their school programs as active or interactive because facilitators use objects or ask questions in their programs. Yes, you can have students do a scavenger hunt or ask them a question while they are watching a PowerPoint presentation, but we need to be honest with ourselves—how *active* are students in these situations? Are they fully *engaged* with the activity? "We want students to grapple with problems," writes Sarah Kuhn, professor emerita of psychology at the University of Massachusetts Lowell, "to question, to think through what a term or a concept means, rather than to see themselves as passive receptacles into which the [guide] pours her wisdom. But [activities] rarely entail physical action beyond writing in a notebook or on a worksheet."[3] This chapter examines techniques for physical, emotional, and social engagement and ways in which school programs and tours can fully engage students with the history of slavery.

Physical Engagement

Physical engagement (also called kinesthetic learning) is the process of using physical activities to stimulate learning.[4] As Beverly Sheppard notes, it plays an important role in museums:

> Our children live in a world with lots of information but little encounter. Few have much experience with how things work, how they are made, or how extraordinary it is to create something of value with their own hands. Museums remain one of the few environments where encounter is the basis of learning.[5]

Our institutions are places where young people can experience, or in Sheppard's words, encounter, learning in a multi-modal fashion. We excel at putting visitors in situations where they literally come face-to-face, and hand-to-object, with history, providing them different ways to engage with the content.

While museums' and historic sites' school programs often include physical engagement with the tasks of our predecessors—churning butter or carrying buckets of water, for example—we must cautiously employ this strategy when interpreting slavery. We never want any activity to trivialize the experiences of the enslaved. Educators must be hyperaware of giving students the wrong impression about the institution or the people who were bound in it. These activities speak to what life was like during the Colonial and Antebellum periods for poor and middling white people as well as the enslaved, so it is imperative we explain who performed this work for enslaving households. While activities such as hauling water, grinding corn, dipping candles, throwing rice, dyeing indigo, churning butter, and ginning cotton might seem fun today, the enslaved people who performed these tasks did them without pay, all day, every day, with little to no breaks, all while being held against their will. Letting a ten-year-old churn butter for thirty (fun) seconds could be intellectually harming students by giving them a rosy concept of slavery. If you instill the wrong impression of slavery at a young age, students will struggle to comprehend a deeper narrative when they get older.

As Nicole Moore, museum educator and long-time interpreter of the enslaved experience, counsels,

Figure 6.1.   Students use a mortar and pestle at Mount Vernon. Courtesy of the Mount Vernon Ladies' Association.

it has to do with getting [students] to understand the difficulty of the labor, and one way to do that is to experience a small sampling of that. I do not think it is the only way or the best way, but it does allow the audience a physical understanding, which is what some folks need. I found with kids who have the "oh this is fun" mentality, by just asking them if they could do this nonstop for hours and in various weather conditions. Then the tone changes to "Uhhh no, I don't think so." It also helps to outright acknowledge that [students] don't HAVE to do this, but those whose experience they are simulating, for choice of a better word, had to do this or suffer consequences.[6]

Public historian Dr. Bob Beatty agrees with Moore. "There's no 'real' way to do it because the folks doing the activities are not enslaved, so the best we have is to simulate the work/working conditions. The rest has to be left up to the imagination . . . that's the job of interpretation."[7]

We need to expand beyond the traditional, hands-on "work" narrative, as "so often museum educators present enslaved people as workers and not humans, mothers, fathers, children."[8] Enslaved people were pulled from their families to work for the benefit of others, and we cannot ignore those familial bonds, either blood or chosen, that were essential to their being. How can we make tangible the intangible aspects of the life of an enslaved person? How might our physical engagement activities communicate the concepts of family or the importance of storytelling to preserving one's culture? One solution includes incorporating the voices of enslaved people into our physical activities by using their words from their autobiographies, memoirs, and reminiscences.

Expanding beyond work also offers us the opportunity to engage students with stories of agency and acts of resistance. We can shift the prism on the work of enslaved people to see it from the perspective of agency. For example, an enslaved man teaching his son the trade of blacksmithing might be the one opportunity he had to parent his child. Think of the pride a parent takes in the accomplishments of their child. Might an enslaved father have felt that way when his son forged his first horseshoe? We might not be able to say that for sure, but because he was a human being, we cannot deny him the agency of that emotion. Think about how you could reframe your physical activities to see possibilities like that.

Learning is contextual. As we learn new concepts, we fit them into the context of what we already know.[9] We can wrap those hands-on activities in context to help students build meaning. The chores of an enslaved person mean less when they stand alone than when the narrative imbeds them within the context of the bondage and inhumanity of slavery as an institution. Dr. Julia Rose, director of Marietta House Museum, urges us to consider the work of enslaved people within the context of integrity. There is integrity in hard work and pride in the value of a skill (especially a skill that can be parlayed into a paying job when one is free).[10] We cannot assign these emotions to specific enslaved people if we do not have a record of them in their own hand, but we can offer them as a context in the range of human emotions.

As researcher George Hein notes, "Physical involvement is a necessary condition for learning for children, and highly desirable for adults in many situations, but it is not sufficient. All kinesthetic activities must also pass the test of being minds-on—they must provide something to think about as well as something to touch."[11] Do not just use physical activities for the sake of doing something "engaging." You must set all physical activities within the context of slavery.

Contextualizing Hands-On Objects

Objects, even reproductions, are powerful and can provoke emotions we need to acknowledge and discuss with students. An informed approach to using hands-on objects when teaching about slavery is critical. As noted above with physical engagement, objects can also help us tell stories of agency, family, and resistance in addition to stories of work

When using hands-on objects, it is important to remember to place the learner, not educators or guides, at the center of the activity. As Hein reminds us, "Learners are the makers of meaning and knowledge."[12] The theory of constructivist learning, which is the belief that learning happens when learners are actively involved in the process of constructing knowledge and meaning instead of passively receiving information, is essential to the interpretation of slavery. Students are not passive receptors of knowledge. They need their minds and bodies to be actively engaged in their learning, including with hands-on objects. Students should be active, challenged at the appropriate level for their grade/age, to understand what they are learning and why, doing the majority of the talking, and taking the time they need to integrate their new knowledge.[13]

Trying to encapsulate the enslaved experience by handling objects, like holding an okra or a cotton ball, gives us only the slightest insight into the lives of enslaved people. As Callie Hawkins from President Lincoln's Cottage remarked, "Historic sites continue to program on things that are cultural vestiges of slavery (foodways and religion) and don't focus enough on what slavery actually was. This prevents us from gaining empathy. You can 'hold' an okra but can't 'hold' being whipped."[14] It is possible for foodways *demonstrations*—note that a demonstration involves little physical engagement on the students' end—to engender a component of empathy when framed correctly. Many African American interpreters who conduct foodways demonstrations—third-person costumed—provide ample context and social/emotional engagement for audience members.[15]

We have to ask students to engage their mind, as well as their emotional intelligence: "What do you think it was like to cook elaborate meals but not partake of them, knowing the scant rations provided by the enslaver are the extent of the cook's diet? How would those calories provide enough subsistence for all the calories burned during work? And what about not receiving credit for their hard work, and possibly receiving punishment if the enslaver perceived something amiss?" Even with the multisensory nature of a foodways demonstration, the essence of enslavement—constant fear of punishment or being held in dehumanizing bondage—cannot be completely encapsulated in a third-person demonstration or by "holding an okra."[16] We must engage students in making meaning out of their hands-on experiences.

Emotional Engagement

This book makes many references to how emotions connect with and arise from the study of slavery. Our programs should not be designed to provoke, or stoke, a particular emotion, as we have no control over the existing knowledge and emotions that students bring to the situation, which determines how they respond to the content. By discussing a range of emotional content, we are supporting learners' ability to form a deeper understanding of the material.[17] All students will not respond the same way to the same story, content, or object. The following section examines some specific techniques that involve connecting emotions with sensory stimulation and historical objects.

Emotional engagement, Kristian J. Spring and others write, is "students' emotional responses (e.g., attitudes, relationships) to other people, stimulus, and content in the learning environment."[18] Students will respond to emotional stimuli differently depending on their age and life experience. A student can be intellectually and physically mature but may not be at the same emotional maturity as their classmates, which may cause them to respond to a historical narrative differently from their classmates or to not be able to deal with deeply emotional content. It is important to consult current literature on youth emotional development while planning your programs.

One way to emotionally connect to the history is through our senses. We use our five senses to navigate the world, so why not use them to navigate history. Think how the smell of crayons, chocolate chip cookies, or sweaty gym clothes evoke emotional childhood memories of joy, comfort, or anxiety. Slave narratives and other accounts of enslavement are full of robust, sensory descriptions of the past. Sharing with students primary source descriptions of the smelly, dark, and crowded hold of a slave ship or the hot, sweaty, prickly job of picking cotton can engage their imaginations and prompt emotional and empathic engagement with the history. As museum educator D. Lynn McRainey writes, "The senses create a depth and dimension to the past that opens a child's eyes [ears, nose, hands, and mouth] to imagine what a particular place might have been like at a particular moment in time."[19] Creating a multisensory experience—the smell of a wood fire; the coarse feel of Negro cloth (also known as "Lowell cloth"), a cheap, coarse textile made specifically to clothe enslaved people; the sight of endless rows of cotton plants; the sound of a Griot sharing an ancient story—these all create robust context for your slavery interpretation.[20]

Another way to emotionally engage with history is through objects, to which many people form emotional attachments. Think about the items in your home or office that make you happy, comforted, or sorrowful. Historical objects, even reproductions, often prompt the same emotions. "Through close looking," Lovisa Brown and associates argue, "objects themselves can speak in ways that the archive—often silent and full of gaps—may not."[21] At museums and historic sites, these objects are often our only physical connection with the past, and more than likely our only representation of the life of an enslaved person. Social psychologist Sherry Turkle coined the term "evocative object" to capture the special blend of thought and feelings that accompany an intimate relationship with an object.

We find it familiar to consider objects as useful or aesthetic, as necessities or vain indulgences. We are on less familiar ground when we consider objects as companions to our emotional lives or as provocations to thought. The notion of evocative objects brings together these two less familiar ideas, underscoring the inseparability of thought and feeling in our relationship to things. Anything can be a thing to think with, although some things are more provocative, or more productive, than others.[22]

Evocative objects, landscapes, and structures, and so on can help us emotionally engage with the content and actively construct meaning.

The lack of material culture of enslaved people should not prohibit this type of engagement, as nearly every object in the "Big House" or on a plantation would have made its way into an enslaved person's hand at one point or another. The farm or kitchen implements that often stand in for the life of an enslaved person can prompt emotional connections with the lives of the people who used them. We can ask students to imagine what an enslaved person might have thought about a field hoe, a tea set, or a Bible, and by pondering what those objects might have represented to an enslaved person. Buildings and landscapes are also material culture that speak to the lives of the enslaved. Objects such as beads, shells,

Figure 6.2.   Visitors to Philipsburg Manor in Sleepy Hollow, New York, connect with the past by placing their hands on a quern used by enslaved people for grinding wheat. Photo by Guido Jimenez-Cruz, C&G Partners, grant by Historic Hudson Valley.

and other talismans that archaeologists found buried in the foundations of slave dwellings provide a tangible sentimental connection to intangible stories. The use of these items can help build empathy for those who cannot speak for themselves.

Social Engagement

At its essence, learning is a social activity—an exchange of information—listening, speaking, and working together to solve a problem or apply knowledge to a situation.[23] Humans are social animals, so it is unwise to expect students to be quiet and listen intently to everything a tour guide says. Putting students face-to-face with each other in discussion, without screens as intermediaries, helps them to *see* and acknowledge the humanity in one another. Then, when they come face-to-face with historical persons, the ability to see and acknowledge someone's humanity can transcend centuries. While social engagement is both important and necessary, museums must take great care in designing experiences to ensure its effectiveness.

An Interconnected Social Web

One activity from the Rhode Island Historical Society helps students engage with each other while learning about the interconnected web of eighteenth-century society, how people from that era in Rhode Island and Connecticut connected with slavery and the slave trade. Based on outfitting documents and manifests from the 1764 voyage of the Brown brothers' ship *Sally*, the activity has students stand in a circle while twenty of them read off cards in random order that address how businesses and individuals were complicit in slavery and slave trade, without directly enslaving any people. During the activity students pass around a ball of yarn, taking hold of the strand before passing it on, as they read information from the cards.

- The *Sally* carried 1,800 onions. In the eighteenth and nineteenth century, the towns of Wethersfield, Connecticut, and Bristol, Rhode Island, led the way in onion production. Farmers in these towns sold their onions to businesses that outfitted slaving voyages. Onions were used for many medicinal purposes. It is now believed that the Vitamin C content of the onions helped sailors fight off scurvy, which explains why ships carried so many.
- The *Sally* carried seven swivel guns. Swivel guns were found on most ships of this period. Armorers made the guns and sold them to slave ship outfitters. Sailors could pivot these small, mounted cannons to fend off pirates and other attackers. On slave ships they could also be used against slave uprisings and insurrections, as happened on the *Sally*.

The continuous passing of the yarn creates a literal web, and a metaphorical web, of complicity that students can see. When prompted, they discuss how the eighteenth-century society's complicity in slavery barely differs from how contemporary society is complicit in low-wage foreign or child labor that produces our iPhones or our Nike shoes. Linking human rights violations past and present demonstrates how easy it is to aid and abet the infringement of others' human rights. By literally connecting to and engaging in dialogue with each other, students are at the center of the learning experience and are creating their own relevance.

Straight Talk about Role-play and Simulations

Role-play and simulation are two go-to techniques educators use in formal and informal learning environments. Before exploring role-play and simulations in the context of interpreting slavery, let me make a distinction between the two techniques.

Role-playing involves taking on a perspective or persona, usually that of a specific person with a name and background story. Simulations involve an interaction or activity and sometimes require participants to take on first-person roles, but they tend to be generic roles like pioneer (Oregon Trail) or pilot (a flight simulator). For museum educator Michelle Moon, "Roleplaying is a type of perspective-taking and choice-making that can take place within a simulation, though not all simulations include roleplaying. And roleplaying can of course take place outside of a simulation."[24]

Research and experience offer justifications for the use of role-playing and simulations in museum education, including their power as a tool for understanding historical experiences and engaging students, and in making a lasting connection to the subject matter.[25] However, while simulations may offer value for *studying* a historical issue, many experts disagree when it comes to the value and wisdom of simulations as a way for students to experience historical trauma. For example, the Holocaust Museum's identity card technique offers visitors the opportunity to connect with a historical person and learn about their experiences during the Holocaust, but it is neither role-playing nor a simulation. It does not ask visitors to simulate the person's Holocaust experience (e.g., being herded into a gas chamber), or to pretend to be the person on the card.

While some argue the benefit of simulation techniques, Samuel Totten, a leading analyst of historical simulations, concludes that "none of these arguments stand up to close scrutiny" in the case of traumatic history.[26] Role-playing and simulations can be psychologically *harmful*, especially for children. The risk of harm may be especially great for someone from the same demographic as the historically oppressed group. It is more important for us to help students learn about the lives of historically oppressed people rather than put them into the situation where they pretend to be an enslaved person picking cotton or a Jewish person in a concentration camp.

Experiencing intense emotions is risky for any child. "Children have different vulnerabilities to such experiences—vulnerabilities teachers cannot and should not be expected to know," says Ingrid Drake, a psychologist whose child experienced a slavery simulation. Drake argues that teachers lack information about how unsafe these exercises are.[27] There is evidence that even one of the most highly regarded and widely used simulations of racial prejudice, the *Blue Eyes/Brown Eyes* exercise, *does* harm children who participate in it. "The children who were in [the simulation] experienced stress and disengagement for a long time afterwards."[28] Students who were told they were inferior began to behave as though they were, including performing poorly on work. The students designated as superior turned mean-spirited and discriminated against their "inferior" classmates.[29] This is not the type of behavior we want students to simulate, even for a short time.

Do *Not* Do Role-plays or Simulations about Slavery

Yes, you read that heading correctly. I am saying,"No!" to role-play and simulations about slavery. When starting this research, I thought that there might be a glimmer of hope, some magic pedagogical technique, that I could provide to help museums use these activities in their interpretation of slavery. But right out of the gate, in my first tour observation at a historic site, I saw that there was no way these techniques could be anything but harmful to children. These activities trivialize the experience of being enslaved and do more harm than good.

The thought that students can only learn what it was like in the past by dressing up in costume and pretending to be someone else has unfortunately become all too prevalent in our field. Nicole Moore thinks of it as "How to End Up on the News 101." These exercises inflict emotional harm on students, are often done without parental permission, and are led by unskilled facilitators who have not thought through the pedagogical techniques or emotional consequences. Bottom line, role-play and simulation will never provide students with the realities of an enslaved person's life.[30]

An immersive experience of being crowded in the hold of a slave ship, worked under threat of a whip, or fleeing for freedom, even when designed with the utmost care, can risk leaving children feeling as though slavery was not so bad after all. In fact, Totten and Feinberg found that all too often, students end up laughing about the simulation, or mocking students of color or those assigned to role-play the enslaved.[31] Role-playing and simulation exercises belittle the subject matter and experts question whether students can actually experience what historical figures did, and whether they are likely to believe that they have, causing them to drastically underestimate historical reality.[32] "[The] simplification of reality can," Totten posits, "lead to a facile understanding of complex issues and, worse still, a trivialization."[33] In addition, how genuinely *real* can you make a simulation that will not trick people into thinking that they really know what it was like? The more or less real a simulation gets, the more confusing it can be.[34]

Many simulations place students in a historical thinking catch-22. In order to truly understand the story, they "must remain connected to the historical situation (seeking refuge on an underground railroad simulation), but in order for that understanding to be valid, they must disconnect themselves from that situation and hold in mind the viewpoints of historical agents (the enslaved)."[35] Historian Tyson Retz captures this paradigm by unpacking Sam Wineburg's work *Historical Thinking and Other Unnatural Acts*. To humanize history we must be able to locate ourselves within a familiar past where we can "tie our stories to those who came before us" (e.g., cooking is something we all do, therefore I can identify with a historical cooking demonstration). Conversely, in order to truly understand history (in this case, slavery), we must "penetrate a strange past where detached from present-day concerns and needs, distant forms of meaning and modes of thought can expand our conceptions of human experience, its limitations and possibilities, and our place within it."[36] In other words, when in a simulation or role-play, we must simultaneously immerse ourselves in the experience yet maintain a thirty-thousand-foot perspective on the past, which is hard for an adult to do, let alone a ten-year-old.

An Oversimplification of Oppression

Many museums default to role-play or simulations as a way to interpret the past, especially when a task or concept radically differs from the contemporary reality of visitors. This stance is particularly concerning when talking about challenging history. Hypothetically, people would be outraged if a school trip to the Auschwitz-Birkenau Memorial and Museum included a simulation of being separated from classmates while some were sent to gas chambers and others to a labor camp to make Nazi missiles. The goal might be empathy, but traumatizing students into empathizing with Holocaust victims/survivors in that manner is not going to help them relate on a personal level. If anything, it might even traumatize students to the point of shutting down altogether, and they might leave with gross misunderstandings of the complexity of the Holocaust. Likewise, the complexity of the history of slavery, and the lives of those who were enslaved, are far too intricate and sensitive to be reduced to a simulation.

> By their very nature, simulations are purposely toned down to make them easier for students to grasp. . . . Such simulations can also degenerate into a time of "play" that is bereft of real thinking. In the end, students often remember the excitement of the game to the exclusion of the intended meaning of the exercise or its relationship to the history under examination.[37]

In the context of historical oppression, there is also the danger that role-playing or simulation reinforces negative stereotypes rather than fostering empathy with the oppressed.[38] Students with existing negative views of historical figures, like enslaved people of African descent or Jewish people, can find historical simulations reinforce or give voice to their existing beliefs.

A 2015 study of a nonhistorical simulation about blindness reported that subjects participating in an exercise involving navigating with a blindfold found participants developed negative stereotypes about the abilities and feelings of people who are blind, rather than achieving the goal of increased empathy for people with low/no vision. Participants even tended to feel that people without sight must live lives of misery, projecting their own experience at being briefly and superficially thrust into darkness onto those who have learned to adapt to their challenge.[39] It seems that a balanced understanding of the challenges faced by other people, including *their* own responses to *their* circumstances, may come from learning *about* someone's life more than from trying to walking a mile in their shoes.[40]

For all of these reasons, interpreters and educators should avoid role-playing and simulations for slavery or other traumatic history. Facing History and Ourselves, a national social justice organization based in Massachusetts that serves 1.6 million students annually, avoids including simulations in its antiracism and anti-Semitism curriculum. In the context of the

Holocaust, the Anti-Defamation League has issued a warning to educators that simulations "can reinforce negative views of the victims."[41]

Additionally, there is the danger that the vivid nature of the simulation will predominate in the minds of learners. While it is important to know the horrors of slavery, and vital to empathize with the enslaved, students should not magnify their experience to the extent that the oppressiveness of slavery dominates their recollection of the historical experiences of African Americans. Students need to see the breadth, depth, and multi-dimensionality of African American experiences in the United States—from slavery and the Civil Rights Movement to accomplishments in a variety of fields like business, agriculture, education, medicine, sports, politics, and entertainment. It is difficult enough to strike an appropriate balance between teaching the centrality of slavery to the American experience and accurately depicting the Black experience as being about far more than just slavery, without ensuring that the painful and traumatic aspects of slavery are what remain most vividly in the minds of learners.

Roles versus Reality

When museums engage students in role-playing a real (or composite) historical person during a tour or program, they may participate in a variety of activities, including dressing up in reproduction clothing, performing period tasks, and reading quotations in a first-person voice. These types of role-play mostly produce negative results, even if students are assigned roles randomly, as the lines between past and present, and reality and fiction, blur for them. Even if told not to, a student may read or speak in dialect or a fake accent, which can go wrong in so many ways. Additionally, unlike classroom teachers, museum educators do not know the students well and see them for a very short time, and therefore they are in the difficult position of not being able to adequately prepare and debrief the role-play with students.

This was evident in a program at Historic London Town and Gardens. In the introduction, a tour guide told the twelve fourth-grade students, comprising an equal combination of Asian, Asian-Indian, and white identities, they would each play the role of someone who lived in the eighteenth century. Upon entering a basement room in the Brown House, once a tavern, the guide told boys and girls to line up separately. The tour guide made the binary decision of who went where and did not give students a choice as to which gender role they wanted to adopt. He gave students costumes—simple homespun shirts for enslaved people, fancy suit coats for wealthy planters, and so on. As the students donned their costumes, I overheard one student say to another, "You're a slave. I can own you now. You're probably a slave because you're wearing this," while pointing to the homespun shirt the student was wearing.[42]

This encounter reflects a myriad of concerns with role-playing. Situations like this might have been avoided altogether by not having students wear reproduction clothing. Donning historical, often inaccurate, reproduction clothing is a bedrock learning activity for countless museums. It is a way that educators try to get students to connect with the past and gain some empathy for historical people. However, as in this example, the students immediately gleaned a dichotomy in the relationships between their historical personages because of the type of clothing they wore. This is no different from assumptions students make today about their classmates based on the type of clothing they are wearing (e.g., designer labels, hand-me-downs, etc.) Kids have a keen sense of what separates themselves from others. In this case, the student used his prior knowledge to discern that a simple shirt must mean that person was a "slave" and his fancy coat made him someone rich and important. These students could have easily gotten trapped in the oppressor/oppressed dichotomy, which makes the situation about dominating each other in the now. This paradigm obfuscates the desire to have students empathize with enslaved Africans and examine the oppressor/oppressed binary of the past. Dress-up is a tempting activity for nine- and ten-year-old students, as they are still of an age when they will use their imaginations and are willing to try almost anything. But, as in this example, it is not appropriate for the topic of slavery.

A slight alteration in approach is much more effective. The guide could lead a close examination of reproduction historical clothing and discuss how much it reveals about people and their lives. He could ask students to look at and feel clothing representing the different social statuses and jobs people had in relation to the time and place in history, followed by a discussion of how enslaved men and women would have had different clothing requirements based on their station and job. An enslaved butler's livery is going to be distinct from an enslaved field worker's shift and breeches, for example. Ask students to describe what they see, make observations, and generate a hypothesis about the clothing. Then link the clothing to the story of an enslaved person at your site. By putting the clothing in context, and by prompting a multisensory exploration, students can emotionally engage with the people and history. Students can connect with and gain empathy for real people, instead of pretending to be someone they are not and missing the point of the activity entirely.

When it comes to role-playing enslaved people and enslavers, the students at Historic London Town were simply too young to deal with the confusing emotions that come with being told to assume roles of power and oppression. This was apparent as their comments and physical discomfort continued throughout the tour. In the tavern's dining room, the tour guide pointed at students (using the costume as a reference) and said, "You are [name]," and proceeded to talk about that person's role in eighteenth-century London Town. When he referenced Bett and Jacob, who were enslaved to the Browns, the students giggled uncomfortably as two of their classmates were singled out as "Bett" and "Jacob." Because the stories the tour guide shared about Bett and Jacob were humanizing and highlighted episodes of agency, it is unclear what was gained by pointing at a student and saying, "You are Bett." A better tack would be to describe Bett's life and ask the students to respond to it—that puts the focus on Bett's life, not on the student uncomfortably dressed in a homespun shift.

Later in the tour, when the guide was telling the story of George Cock, an enslaved sailor, the student he pointed to was visibly uncomfortable being singled out, pouting and crossing his arms over his chest in a protective gesture as his classmates glared and giggled at him. When passing to the next stop on the tour, another student said to him, "You're enslaved." The students never got to read or talk about anything associated with George. They were not asked to imagine what Bett or George might have felt in a particular situation. Thus, students were completely disconnected from the humanity of the enslaved.

In a post-tour discussion with the guide, I asked about the wearing of costumes as a learning technique. He responded that they did not want students to role-play slaves, so he avoided saying "You are a slave" to students. I noted that by him pointing to a costumed student and referring to him by the name of an enslaved person, he was essentially doing the very thing that he was trying to avoid. While he acknowledged the goal was to use stories of real people to bring humanity to the history, unfortunately, the activity was not designed to account for students' feelings of discomfort or inappropriate reactions to dressing in costume. I do not believe he was intentionally trying to do harm, but the design of the activity reflects a lack of understanding of appropriate pedagogical techniques, how tours/tour guides can inflict trauma on young people, and how frontline staff carry out the directives of the administration without having proper training to fall back on. By not realizing what happened with this group, that they may have inadvertently caused emotional harm, the staff may be causing students to associate museums with being made to feel bad about themselves. Situations like this can build a young person's distrust in historic sites that can last for years.

During this post-tour discussion, another tour guide added that they avoided telling "happy stories," like the one of an enslaved person who ran away, so as to not to give the impression that there were many who ran away when the majority did not.[43] Yes, not every enslaved person tried to run or fight back, but just telling stories of misery and beatings is wrong and dangerously misleading. We must not perpetuate a single story of slavery, but instead we must help students interrogate the complexities of the institution.[44] Stories of agency portray enslaved people in a positive light and interrupt traditional narratives of suffering and trauma. It is therefore critical to share the real details of the lives of enslaved people. For them to not share the empowering story of an enslaved person who self-emancipated is a tremendous oversight. (See chapter 1 about historical trauma.)

It is impossible to quantify the emotional damage (if any) of this encounter for the students who were singled out—by their peers or the tour guide—as representing enslaved people in the activity. However, students left with a narrow, negatively weighted picture of those who were enslaved at London Town. If a museum does not offer historical context and a proper debrief activity, students may leave with a one-dimensional understanding of enslaved lives and possibly even with new trauma of their own.

Engaging students physically and emotionally with history is one of the most important things museum educators do. Meaningful engagement is the only way students truly learn. Whether we are using sensory stimuli, hands-on objects, or primary sources, it is important to help students find their own relevance in, and make their own meaning of, the history. Actively engaging them with historical people and narratives can help them build deeper understandings and a desire to seek additional information. As Suzanne MacLeod and associates. write, "Sites which invite [students] to piece together the history themselves, within a clear narrative framework, have been suggested to unite the cognitive and affective domains because they invite questions, reflection, and provide opportunities for critical thinking and enquiry-based learning."[45] As noted, role-play and simulations have no place in museum education programs about slavery. The chance of inflicting trauma on young people is too great. If the activity devolves into play, we trivialize the history and historical people, and students miss the point altogether. By designing programs that engage students with the historical narrative and real historical people, we provide them with an opportunity to find relevance in the past.

Notes

1. Elie Wiesel, "Then and Now: The Experiences of a Teacher," *Social Education* 42 (1978): 266–71.
2. Ed Rodley, "Defining Engagement," Thinking about Museums, December 4, 2019; accessed, November 11, 2020, https://thinkingaboutmuseums.com/2019/12/04/defining-engagement/.
3. Sarah Kuhn, *Thinking with Things: Remaking Learning in College and Beyond* (unpublished manuscript, March 2018), 18.
4. "Student Engagement," *The Glossary of Education Reform*, accessed November 10, 2018, https://www.edglossary.org/student-engagement/?fbclid=IwAR1fSglHCluJiieXqjv-G4E34fy_EQZY8YNazWeXJDF9DLpYtnGYeDA5YW4.
5. Jamie Credle, "Endless Possibilities: Historic House Museum Programs That Make Educators Sing," in *Interpreting Historic House Museums*, ed. Jessica Foy Donnelly (Walnut Creek, CA: AltaMira Press, 2002), 272.
6. Nicole Moore, Facebook reply to the author's inquiry, June 18, 2017.
7. Dr. Bob Beatty, Facebook reply to the author's inquiry, June 18, 2017.
8. Dr. Julia Rose, conversation with the author, November 8, 2020.
9. George Hein, "Constructivist Learning Theory," accessed March 16, 2018, http://beta.edtech policy.org/AAASGW/Session2/const_inquiry_paper.pdf .
10. Dr. Julia Rose, conversation with the author, November 8, 2020.
11. Hein, "Constructivist Learning Theory."
12. Hein, "Constructivist Teaching Methods," accessed March 16, 2018, https://en.wikipedia .org/wiki/Constructivist_teaching_methods.
13. Hein, "Constructivist Learning Theory," accessed November 15, 2020, https://www.exploratorium.edu/education/ifi/constructivist-learning; and Emily Liebtag," 8 Things to Look for in a Student-Centered Learning Environment," Getting SMART, August 9, 2017; accessed November 15, 2020, https://www.gettingsmart.com/2017/08/8-things-look-student-centered -learning-environment/.
14. Callie Hawkins, interview with the author, March 24, 2017.
15. Nicole Moore, Dontavious Williams, Cheyney McKnight, and Michael Twitty are just a few of the African American public historians who provide emotionally and intellectually engaging, historically accurate foodways demonstrations.
16. White women in historic costume leading cooking demonstrations in a kitchen on a plantation that was historically helmed by an enslaved cook is a misrepresentation of reality and not sound interpretation. See Kelley Fanto Deetz, "Memo from a Historian: White Ladies Cooking in Plantation Museums Are a Denial of History," The Conversation, December 13, 2019, https://theconversation.com/memo-from-a-historian-white-ladies-cooking-in-plantation -museums-are-a-denial-of-history-127797.
17. See the work of Stacey Mann and Danny M. Cohen, including "When a Boxcar Isn't a Boxcar: Designing for Human Rights Learning," https://www.academia.edu/986543/When_a_Boxcar_Isn_t_a_Boxcar_Designing_for_Human_Rights_Learning_Exhibition _Fall_2011_reproduced_with_permission_; and "Crying at the Museum: A Call for Responsible Emotional Design," https://www.academia.edu/35359205/Crying_At_the_Museum _A_Call_for_Responsible_Emotional_Design_Exhibition_Spring_2017_reproduced _with_permission_.

18. Kristian J. Spring et al., "Learner Engagement in Blended Learning," *IGI Global*, accessed November 10, 2018, https://www.igi-global.com/chapter/learner-engagement-in-blended-learning/183863.

19. D. Lynn McRainey, "A Sense of the Past," *Connecting Kids to History Museum Exhibits*, ed. D. Lynn McRainey and John Russick (Walnut Creek, CA: Left Coast Press, 2010), 161.

20. Modern linsey-woolsey or Osnaburg fabrics can simulate Negro cloth.

21. Lovisa Brown, Caren Gutierrez, Janine Okmin, and Susan McCullough, "Desegregating Conversations about Race and Identity in Culturally Specific Museums," *Journal of Museum Education* 42, no. 2 (May 2017): 123.

22. Sherry Turkle, ed. *Evocative Objects: Things We Think With* (Cambridge, MA: MIT Press, 2011), 5.

23. Hein, "Constructivist Learning Theory."

24. Michelle Moon, Facebook communication with the author, February 1, 2019.

25. The Tsongas Industrial History Center conducts the popular Workers on the Line program, in which students "work" on an assembly line—with all the vicissitudes of speed-ups, pay cuts, and layoffs—in order to gain insight into the experience of 1840s textile workers. Former student visitors still have vivid memories of their assembly-line experience many years later.

26. Samuel Totten, "Diminishing the Complexity and Horror of the Holocaust: Using Simulations in an Attempt to Convey Historical Experiences," *Social Education* 64, no.3 (April 2000): 165–71.

27. Ingrid Drake, "Classroom Simulations: Proceed with Caution," *Teaching Tolerance*, accessed February 22, 2019, https://www.tolerance.org/magazine/spring-2008/classroom-simulations-proceed-with-caution. Compare with Simone A. Schweber, "Simulating Survival," *Curriculum Inquiry*, accessed February 22, 2019, https://website.education.wisc.edu/sschweber/pub_pdfs/CURI3art.pdf. Schweber acknowledges the risks of simulating traumatic history, including psychological harm, trivializing the history, and encouraging empathy with perpetrators rather than victims. Schweber is, nevertheless, optimistic about such simulations but bases this optimism simply on observing one classroom simulation of the Holocaust, over an extended period of time, without any attempt to show that the instructor or the simulation design are typical or to evaluate the children for signs of psychological stress.

28. Melanie Killen, developmental psychologist, quoted in Drake, "Classroom Simulations."

29. "A Class Divided," Frontline, January 1, 2003; accessed October 2, 2020, https://www.pbs.org/wgbh/frontline/article/introduction-2/.

30. Nicole Moore, note to the author, September 6, 2020.

31. See, for example, Samuel Totten and Stephen Feinberg, "Teaching about the Holocaust," accessed February 22, 2019, http://www.socialstudies.org/sites/default/files/publications/se/5906/590601.html.

32. As Totten puts it in "Diminishing the Complexity," "To suggest that one can approximate even a scintilla of what its victims went through is sheer folly." He adds, "What is of critical importance here is that the use of such simulations often results in students believing that—at least to some extent—they do." Or in the words of Totten and Feinberg, "Teaching about the Holocaust," "Simply put, there is absolutely no way a student can ever experience what the victims of the Holocaust lived through, and it is pedagogically unsound to even attempt a simulation for such purposes."

33. Totten, "Diminishing the Complexity and Horror of the Holocaust: Using Simulations in an Attempt to Convey Historical Experiences."

34. Andrea Jones, interview with the author, March 2, 2018.
35. Tyson Retz, *Empathy and History: Historical Understanding in Re-enactment, Hermeneutics and Education* (New York, Oxford: Berghahn Books, 2018), 66.
36. Retz, *Emphathy and History*.
37. Totten and Feinberg, "Teaching about the Holocaust."
38. Totten and Feinberg, "Teaching about the Holocaust." See also Drake, "Classroom Simulations."
39. Arielle M. Silverman, Jason D. Gwinn, and Leaf Van Boven, "Stumbling in Their Shoes: Disability Simulations Reduced Judged Capabilities of Disabled People," *Social Psychology and Personality Science* 6, no. 4 (May 2015): 464–71.
40. See Sam Wineburg, *Historical Thinking and Other Unnatural Acts*. "Historical thinking requires us to reconcile two contradictory positions: first, that our established modes of thinking are an inheritance that cannot be sloughed off; second, that if we make no attempt to slough them off, we are doomed to a mind-numbing presentism that reads the present onto the past."
41. Drake, "Classroom Simulations."
42. Historic London Town, tour observation by Kristin Gallas, March 22, 2017.
43. Historic London Town, staff interview with Kristin Gallas, March 22, 2017.
44. For more information on the potential harm of oversimplified narratives, watch "The Danger of a Single Story" by Chimamanda Ngozi Adichie, TED Global, 2009, accessed October 3, 2020, https://www.ted.com/talks/chimamanda_ngozi_adichie_the_danger_of_a_single_story/transcript?language=en.
45. Suzanne MacLeod et al., *Prisoners, Punishment, and Torture: Developing New Approaches to Interpretation at the Tower of London* (London: Research Centre for Museums and Galleries in the School of Museum Studies at the University of Leicester and Historic Royal Palaces, 2014), 16.

CHAPTER 7

Dialogue Techniques

"Questions are designed to probe, to find something that is not already there, to discover relationships and possibilities that are not given."[1] —Matthew H. Bowker

L EARNING IS a social activity, and social engagement employs a variety of approaches to stimulate learning through communal interactions.[2] For students, learning together is another way to construct meaning, and it happens in the mind and out loud. By engaging students in dialogue, they hear and share different points of view, and can decide for themselves what pieces are most relevant to them.

Our content must inspire students to think critically, both before and *as* they speak. The tried-and-true "think, pair, share" method in which students think about what they want to say, talk it over with a partner, and then share with the larger group, is a simple construct that eases them into examining their thoughts and those of their peers. Another effective strategy to get students thinking is by asking open-ended (i.e., questions that cannot be answered yes or no, or with a specific answer), thought-provoking questions that spur dialogue and help contextualize hands-on activities. The key in all of this is to employ tactics to get young people talking and processing the information they have learned at your museum or site. This chapter examines several techniques for engaging students in dialogue about slavery.

Questioning Techniques

"How much does this bale of cotton weigh?" "How early did the cook have to wake up?" If you have ever asked questions like this, stop now. A school program is not a test of students' knowledge. These questions do not lead anywhere; they simply presume students already know the answer. Instead, tour guides and interpreters must be dialogue facilitators, using questions that spark conversation and social interaction. To do this correctly, we must show respect for the students' thoughts and perspectives, and we can do that with shared authority.[3] By asking open-ended questions and allowing students to be the authority—or teacher—on something they are knowledgeable about, we open ourselves up to be learners.

Today, young people are used to engaging in serious conversations via social media, where they share their thoughts to connect with others. Let's open up our school programs to allow them to talk through their connections with the history and with each other.

Most students are not going to be experts on antebellum American slavery, but they are experts on their own thoughts and emotions, which can help them make connections with the lives of the people of the past. The ideal way to do this is to stop talking and start listening. By asking our students to participate in the interpretive process, we can prompt their thinking and help them make connections.

Stop the Guessing Game and Start Encouraging Critical Thinking

We want students to think critically about the history, and to do that we need to set them up with appropriate questions. I was once given a piece of great advice about questioning techniques, "If you want a student to know something, just tell them." This is perfect advice for the museum educator who wastes time asking closed-ended questions, especially with students who may not have the knowledge or context to guess the answer that you want them to say. Can *you* tell how much a bale of cotton weighs just by looking at it? It is insulting and demoralizing for a student to make a guess, only to be told their answer was wrong. The weight of a bale is not as important as *why* the students should care about the weight. Instead of asking about weight, an educator might say,

> This cotton bale weighs 500 pounds. Before the invention of the cotton gin, an enslaved person could hand-pick the seeds from only one pound of cotton per day. Imagine being faced with the prospect of hand-picking seeds from 500 pounds of cotton. Try pulling the seeds out of this tiny piece of cotton—what is that like? How do you think an enslaved person might have felt about the prospect of hand-picking the seeds from this entire bale?

There are also what I call tricky questions, or questions that just miss the mark, such as "We no longer have slaves to do our work. Why?" or "How was this space [a slave cabin] used?" The educator who developed these questions was trying to create open-ended questions, but the execution was lacking. The questions did not set students up for success. A better question that gets to the same core concepts as the first question above is "What do you think our country would be like if slavery had never been legal in the United States?" This asks students to think critically about the institution of slavery and its effects on the social, political, and economic foundations of the United States.

In the case of the second question, it is always helpful to first give students a frame of reference for what they are seeing. Most students have never even visited a farm, so to query the purpose of a small, abandoned cabin is probably beyond what they already know. Instead, you might ask, "What do you think it would have been like to live in this small cabin with eight other people?" or "What objects do you see here and what might they tell us about what life might have been like for the enslaved people who lived here?" These questions give students a frame of reference for how enslaved people used the space (as a living space) and its significance (as home for enslaved people).

Some questions seem thought provoking on the surface, but obscure deeper, unintended messages. For example, how many times have you heard or asked this question: "Would you have wanted to work in the house or in the fields?" The first time I heard this question was from a National Park Service colleague. She, an African American woman, had been on tour at a historic site and the guide had asked the question of the group. My colleague responded, "Neither, because it would mean that I was enslaved. And by asking that question you're implying that enslaved people had a choice." I am pretty sure that is not the answer the tour guide was expecting. In addition to implying that enslaved people had autonomy over their work choices, the question also suggests that some duties were better than others and plays into the stereotype that "house slaves" were better than "field slaves."

If historic site staff wanted students to think critically about the responsibilities and liabilities of slavery and the agency certain jobs afforded some enslaved people, they could take a more nuanced approach. In doing so, they paint the lives of enslaved people with colorful detail, instead of the proverbial broad brush, highlighting an individual's humanity, triumphs, and tragedies. Enslaved people's responsibilities, liabilities, and agency can be gleaned from primary sources. Students can analyze sources to extract information about the day-to-day tasks of the enslaved, including their liabilities (burdens) and any authority they had over their lives. For example, students can compare these descriptions of the lives of two men enslaved by George Washington.

William Lee, Enslaved Manservant to George Washington

Extracted from "Enslaved People at Mount Vernon" and related primary sources.[4]

RESPONSIBILITIES	LIABILITIES[5]	AGENCY
• Delivering messages • Laying out Washington's clothes • Shaving Washington's face and styling his hair • Organizing the general's personal affairs, including his voluminous papers • Holding his spyglass	• Spent the entirety of the Revolutionary War and early federal period separated from his family • Sleeping in the same room/tent as, or immediately adjacent to, Washington • Married a free woman of color in Philadelphia, but was separated from her when Lee returned to Mount Vernon • Wore easily identifiable Washington livery	• Traveled all over the country while in service to Washington • Privy to GW's private conversations with generals and politicians • Accomplished horseman • Received specialized health care at GW's behest • Emancipated upon GW's death and given an annual allowance of $30 for the rest of his life

Davy Gray, Enslaved Overseer on George Washington's Muddy Hole Farm

Extracted from "Enslaved People at Mount Vernon" and related primary sources[6]

RESPONSIBILITIES	LIABILITIES	AGENCY
• Supervising day-to-day operations of the field work • Reporting to the plantation manager • Ensuring that other enslaved workers performed their assigned duties thoroughly and attentively	• Was an enslaved man giving orders to other enslaved people • Had to administer punishments to enslaved workers who did not perform to expectations • Davy was a "dower slave," part of Martha's property; therefore, he was not emancipated at Washington's death	• Lived with his enslaved wife Molly • Received praise from Washington for carrying on "his business as well as the white overseers, and with more quietness than any of them. With proper directions he will do very well." • Given leather breeches, occasional cash gifts, and extra quantities of pork • Advocated to Washington on behalf of his fellow enslaved workers

When students have this information, they can more analytically contrast William Lee's and Davy Gray's lives. A tour guide could ask, "How do you think William Lee's and Davy Gray's responsibilities affected the liabilities and agency in their lives? How might that have affected their personalities, sense of self, emotional well-being, and interactions with other enslaved people or white people?"

What Makes a Good Open-Ended Question?

There are many different types of open-ended questions that can facilitate different types of thoughtful, sustained discussions, including the following:[7]

- Analysis: Questions beginning with "Why do you think . . . ?," "How would you explain . . . ?," "What do you think is the importance of . . . ?," or "What does [this topic, concept, etc.] mean to you?"
  - Example: "What do you think was the original meaning of the phrase 'all men are created equal' and who was it meant for? How has the meaning evolved over the past two hundred years? What does it mean today?"
- Compare and Contrast: "What do you see as the differences between . . . ?" or "What do you see are the similarities between . . . ?"
  - Example: "What do you see as the differences between the living conditions of a person enslaved at Washington's mansion house and those of an enslaved person on his Dogue Run farm? How may those conditions have affected the lives of those enslaved at each site?"

- Cause and Effect: "What do you think are the causes/results of . . . ?" or "What connections do you see between . . . ?"
  - Example: "What connections can you make between the public sensationalism of Mark Codman's trial and hanging for murdering his enslaver and the public extra-judicial lynchings of the 1950s?"

Responding to Students

I liken interpretation and presenting programs to improvisation. I know the setting and the players and have an idea of where I would like to go, but how we get there is different every time based on who is in the group. The main rule of improvisation is to say, "Yes, and." Accept what your partner has given you and move the scene forward by giving him or her something to respond to. This is where the well-honed skills of a facilitator come into play. It is not enough to know how to ask good open-ended questions but museum educators must also know how to listen and respond to a student's answer in a way that moves the dialogue forward. This is the improvisation.

This improvisation means our job is not complete when we ask a question. If an open-ended question elicits one-word answers from students, prompt them with additional questions. It can be as simple as asking "Why?" or "Would you tell us more?" Following up on one-word answers shows students that you value what they are saying, while also prompting them to think more critically about the matter at hand. Complex topics such as slavery necessitate a nuanced narrative, requiring students and museum educators to share the thought behind their words. "We should not and cannot allow students to package such complex issues and causes neatly into one-word answers,"[8] Scott M. Waring, professor of social studies education at the University of Central Florida writes. This concept is akin to the "show your work" concept in mathematics. By asking students to answer in more than one word, we encourage them to explain how they came to their conclusion and elaborate on it. It is making thinking visible. Through their research, the staff of Project Zero have found that

> when thinking is visible . . . students are in a position to be more metacognitive, to think about their thinking. Teachers benefit when they can see students' thinking because misconceptions, prior knowledge, reasoning ability, and degrees of understanding are more likely to be uncovered. Teachers can then address these challenges and extend students' thinking by starting from where they are.[9]

The only way for us to understand student visitors, and help them understand the history we present, is to ask them to share themselves with us and provide them with the brave space to do so. Open-ended questions and skillful follow-up questions are one way to help them connect with the content.

Help Students Ask Better Questions

Appropriate questions are a vital part of learning. Matthew H. Bowker, who researches the pedagogy of teaching and learning, argues, "The problem today isn't that we don't have the answers, but that we don't have the questions."[10] Yes, museum educators can model good questioning techniques for students, but it is not enough for just us to ask questions. Questions are especially important in helping students think critically about the history of slavery and we must encourage them to ask thoughtful, probing questions as well. Students should be able to engage with the historic resources, content, and each other by asking questions. If staff encourage questions, students exercise their curiosity, make connections to the content, and find relevance. In our brief time with student visitors, it is imperative that we reinforce this important skill. For example,

1. *Start with a question*: You might start out your tour/program by looking at a key image, object, or historic structure related to your content and ask students, "What questions might you have about . . . ?" This allows you to gauge where students are in their journey of acquiring and processing knowledge about the topic.

2. *Wonder aloud*: If there is a piece of content or historic event that you have questions about, model that curiosity for your students. If we put intention behind our musings, we could encourage a whole program of "I wonder" statements. We may not always come up with answers, but thinking aloud prompts others to think aloud, prompting additional questions that may be answered later. You may say, "I've always wondered what would have happened if Belinda Sutton (enslaved by Loyalist Isaac Royall in pre–Revolutionary War Massachusetts) had received the full reparations awarded to her by the state legislature. How would her life have turned out differently? What would you want to ask Belinda if you could talk with her?"

3. *Turn questions back on the student*: When students ask questions that are answerable with information they can glean by making observations of their surroundings, or by simply thinking critically about the content, turn the question back on them. If a student asks, "If he was a free man, why didn't Solomon Northup just run away from the Ford plantation or why didn't he tell a police officer?" Instead of answering, you could ask the student, "Imagine what it was like for Solomon. He was hundreds of miles away from home in a part of the country he did not know, in a place where the law said that everyone who looked like him was enslaved. How might all those restrictions on his freedom have affected his decision making?"

These types of techniques are essential to encourage critical thinking skills and help them increase their abilities to empathize with historical actors.

Incorporating Dialogue into an Activity

Opportunities for questions, reflection, and discussion are not merely occasions for learners to process new information. It is also a way to encourage dialogue. A 2011 study in the United

Kingdom found that when teachers focused on student input in conversations, students were actively and effectively engaged in learning. "[When] children participated more in conversations, there was evidence of children connecting their ideas together giving more of a genuine dialogue. Children increased the time spent extending the ideas of themselves and other children."[11] Dialogue offers students a chance to process individually and collectively by listening to the thoughts of others, talking through different ideas, seeking reassurance, and perhaps most importantly, expressing emotions and observing the emotional reactions of others.

I observed this type of dialogue-reflection activity during a school field trip at President Lincoln's Cottage. The activity was structured on the Arc of Dialogue, which pairs a common experience shared by all participants with a sequence of questions designed to build trust and communication, allowing participants to interact in more relevant and personal ways.[12] (See box 7.1 for details.) During the visit, students toured the home and learned about Lincoln's long journey to drafting the Emancipation Proclamation. The staff helped students empathize with the struggles of those enslaved in the past, the legacies of slavery in the United States, and the plight of those caught up in modern-day slavery. The group of eighth-grade students, sixteen white and one African American, was from a Washington, DC–area private school. The final part of the program had students standing in a circle and simply passing around a ball of yarn—unspooling it as they went, with each student taking hold of the yarn before passing the ball to another—as they responded to a series of prompts. The act of sharing their answers while passing the ball of yarn, and maintaining a hold on the unwound part, created a physical and metaphorical web, an interconnected network of ideas. The first prompt the museum educator gave them was "Name a good quality about yourself." The students did not take this part of the activity seriously, laughing and talking among themselves. Many students were not paying attention and missed the ball of yarn when it was tossed at them.

Box 7.1   The Arc of Dialogue

There are four phases to the Arc of Dialogue:[13]

Phase One—*Build Community*: Encourages connectedness and relationship-building within the group by creating a space where all participants can engage.

Phase Two—*Sharing Our Own Experiences*: Invites participants to think about and share their own experiences with the topic.

Phase Three—*Exploring beyond Our Own Experiences*: Provokes participants to dig deeper into their assumptions and to probe underlying social conditions that inform our diversity of perspectives.

Phase Four—*Synthesizing and Closing the Learning Experience*: Reinforces a sense of community by asking questions to help participants examine what they've learned about themselves and each other and voice the impact that the dialogue has had on them.

The educator then asked, "Can anyone make any symbolic idea of what we just did?" One of the students responded, "Even though it's complicated, we're all united by our good qualities," referring to the yarn-web they had created. The educator offered the next prompt, "Name a good quality of someone else in the class." As a passive observer of the group for the previous hour, I honestly thought this activity was going to crash and burn at that moment, but I was pleasantly surprised that the students paid more attention to this prompt. They focused on what they had to say about each other. Summing up this part of the activity, the educator said, "This time we were united by noticing the good qualities of others. It's not enough to notice what's good about yourself, but to notice what is good about others."

Still passing the yarn, the museum educator asked students to name a problem they noticed in the country today. After the students responded, he summed that up with, "Notice how we are tied together by problems. They can affect you or others you know. Now, can you think of any solutions?" Still passing the yarn and very much engaged, the students named a variety of solutions. Then the educator summed up the activity with "You demonstrated why it doesn't work if people aren't focused on what others have to say. We are still fighting the problems like human trafficking, bad schools, racism, and other legacies of slavery."

In their post-visit survey, students noted this activity as the one they were most emotionally moved by during their visit. "It made me realize the country's problems," remarked one. Another reported, "The yarn activity helped me focus on the problems in America and how to fix them." Additionally, they related to the content that connected with their world today, saying, "When [the museum educator] said that there was still many schools with segregation today. It made me feel sorry for how they are treated," "When he said that today people are still enslaved, and it is not all fixed, it inspired me," and "Something he said that moved me was that slavery still exists today."[14]

By helping the students connect their lives to contemporary problems in the United States and around the world, the museum educator prompted awareness and empowered them to see ways they can make changes. We cannot rescue people from the past, but inspired youth can channel those feelings into making productive changes in their world.

When planning out your program, think about how the activity and dialogue will flow from one point to the next. Where are the opportunities for questions or quiet reflective time? Think about how you will get feedback from the students—are there ways other than the traditional question/answer format to solicit their thoughts? And, what happens once the students have been empowered by your discussions? How can they channel their newfound understandings about slavery and race? Perhaps there is an opportunity for a post-visit lesson the teacher can do back in the classroom, or maybe the students generate their own "next steps" as part of your program.

Building dialogue with your students is empowering—for you and for them. It creates a foundation of respect for everyone to construct new knowledge, understanding, and relevance. Through competent facilitation and the use of sound questioning techniques, we can offer students a profound experience to connect with the history and legacies of slavery.

Notes

1. Matthew H. Bowker, "Teaching Students to Ask Questions Instead of Answering Them," accessed March 25, 2018, http://qa11.nea.org/assets/img/PubThoughtAndAction/Bowker short.pdf.

2. "Student Engagement," *The Glossary of Education Reform*, accessed November 10, 2018, https://www.edglossary.org/student-engagement/?fbclid=IwAR1fSglHCluJiieXqjv-G4E34fy_EQZY8YNazWeXJDF9DLpYtnGYeDA5YW4.

3. "Shared authority, a concept articulated by Michael Frisch vis-à-vis oral history some twenty years ago, is employed here to make the case that, in collaborative museum work that aims to be responsive to social needs, all parties involved must be understood to be authorities on topics of value to the collaboration, and must be understood to have the power and position to fully co-create. Operating from a position of shared authority requires that we consider ourselves first and foremost as both educators and learners. We must recognize that we always and already share authority, for we do not have all the answers—or even all the questions. And we need, perhaps more than anything, to be open to engaging in acts of translation in which we seek to understand fully another's voice and perspective and demystify the language that we and others use to talk about what we do." Elizabeth Duclos-Orsello, "Shared Authority: The Key to Museum Education as Social Change," *Journal of Museum Education* 38, no.2 (July 2013): 122.

4. "Enslaved People at Mount Vernon," accessed March 25, 2018, http://www.mountvernon.org/george-washington/slavery/enslaved-people-at-mount-vernon/.

5. By no means am I implying that there was any free will afforded to enslaved people by their enslavers. I am defining liabilities as "exposed or subject to some usually adverse contingency or action." Agency is "the state of being in action or of exerting power." I chose these words to nuance the ways in which enslaved people were trapped in an inhumane institution yet were able to find ways of exercising their humanity.

6. "Enslaved People at Mount Vernon," accessed March 25, 2018, http://www.mountvernon.org/george-washington/slavery/enslaved-people-at-mount-vernon/.

7. "Designing Effective Discussion Questions," accessed May 29, 2021, https://www.bu.edu/teaching-writing/files/2020/03/effectivediscussionquestions.pdf.

8. Scott M. Waring, "Escaping Myopia: Teaching Students about Historical Causality," *The History Teacher* 43, no. 2 (February 2010): 284.

9. "Making Thinking Visible," accessed May 29, 2021, https://www.mtvt.org/resources/making-thinking-visible-with-technology/.

10. Bowker, "Teaching Students to Ask Questions."

11. Kirsty Brown and Hilary Kennedy, "Learning through Conversation: Exploring and Extending Teacher and Children's Involvement in Classroom Talk," *School Psychology International* 32, no. 4 (August 2011): 391.

12. "Facilitated Dialogue," International Coalition of Sites of Conscience, accessed January 29, 2021, https://www.sitesofconscience.org/wp-content/uploads/2019/01/Dialogue-Overview.pdf.

13. "Facilitated Dialogue," International Coalition of Sites of Conscience, accessed January 29, 2021, https://www.sitesofconscience.org/wp-content/uploads/2019/01/Dialogue-Overview.pdf.

14. Post-visit survey comments, President Lincoln's Cottage, March 24, 2017.

CHAPTER 8

Staff Training and Support

"They don't care how much you know until they know how much you care."[1] —Rex Ellis

THE MOST important part of preparing for interpreting slavery with children and teens is comprehensive and conscientious training for your staff. This means *all* staff: educators, curators, administrators, maintenance workers, everyone. Institutions that invest time and resources in training promote a healthy and supportive work environment. Often, training is the compelling difference between an okay experience and an exceptional one. Simply put, improperly trained staff foil the most well-intentioned attempts to interpret the history of slavery with students. Museums and historic site staff must do this work before they can expect to work with young visitors on this challenging history. This chapter presents practical, replicable advice on staff training sourced from colleagues across the field who have served in frontline roles and/or managed frontline staff.

An Organization Is Only as Good as Its Frontline Staff

The composition of frontline staff (tour guides, interpreters, front desk staff, school programs staff, etc.) that interact with students at museums and historic sites varies depending on the organization. They can be full-time positions with benefits; part-time, hourly workers; volunteers; or some combination thereof. Whatever the composition, remember that an institution is only as good as the people who tell its story. They can make or break an organization. You must invest in them, as they are the ones who interact with students on a regular basis.

Museum educators often tell me that they want to be more comfortable talking with students about slavery. This is a mischaracterization of the needed skill set. Remember that slavery is an inherently uncomfortable part of history, and we should hold on to that discomfort to let it guide our work. Otherwise, we become complacent. To talk about a narrative so fraught with emotion, staff must be confident and competent in their abilities to engage with students.

This begins with our hiring processes for staff, paid and unpaid. We should not bring anyone onto the team who is not prepared for, or ready to be trained for, talking about slavery and race. Andrea Jones notes,

> [The education team] are the key to deeper engagement and addressing, with nuance, racial tensions that inevitably enter the museum each day. I'm just not sure we're going get the results we want with a corps of volunteer docents or even part-time educators unless everyone is committed to the training.[2]

As Jones notes, before an organization begins to think about staff training, leadership needs to determine if they will achieve their interpretive goals and desired student experience with volunteers, community reenactors, or underpaid, part-time staff. Touching back on the topic of chapter 2, spend time thinking about how you are defining success. What are your interpretive goals? What type of research and interpretive skills will the frontline staff need to develop and implement programs? For far too long our field has devalued the role of the frontline interpreter/educator, looking upon it as a job that anyone who likes history can do. It is critical to think about the responsibilities you are placing on the frontline staff, what skills they need to have, the emotional toll interpreting slavery takes on them, and how you will compensate them for the complex and challenging job you are asking them to do.

Many sites bemoan the fact that they have an all-white staff. The multi-faceted, complex reality of this situation is that for generations our institutions have not told diverse stories, have been unwelcoming to people of color, have required candidates to hold advanced degrees, and have endured on the work of unpaid interns. Brandon Dillard counsels that we

> must be willing to pay professional interpreters [a living wage] and not just those who can afford to work in a museum for so little pay. The intersectional realities of race, class, and gender in this country primarily relegate such positions to wealthy white people. . . . The realities of racism and sexism that permeate a culture of white male supremacy [in museums] will continue to do so until the field makes substantive changes in hiring practices and wealth allocation.[3]

Additionally, underpaid entry-level, "pay your museum dues" jobs are not sustainable for people who do not have generational wealth or a family safety net.

Museums need to assess their plan for frontline/education staff who work with students. Developing and facilitating school programs about slavery is a great responsibility. Do not consider it a job for just anyone who likes to talk about history. Foremost, it requires a commitment to a diverse narrative, the willingness to examine one's biases, and the ability to help students wrestle with the emotional nature of the content. Structure must follow strategy; therefore, staffing and training models should reflect institutional values and goals. The staffing model must shift as our narratives do.

In 2017 I worked with Salem Maritime National Historical Park (SAMA), in Massachusetts, to develop their values and goals for interpreting the history of free and enslaved

Africans in the community. The leadership team wanted to show their commitment to the work of the frontline staff; therefore, they agreed to a series of tasks to create a more transparent and inclusive work environment, including the following:

1. To conduct processes—interpretive development decisions, hiring procedures, community collaborations, etc.—that are transparent and informed, SAMA management will be clear when interpretive narratives are firm and why, and where there is flexibility and why.
2. To be inclusive, empowering new and diverse narratives and perspectives, historical and contemporary, SAMA managers will make time for staff to do research, and will empower staff to research, find sources, process the content, and create interpretive narratives that align with the SAMA's interpretive goals.
3. To foster a passionate, inspired, and confident staff, all SAMA staff and management will exhibit passion for their work, and a contagious positive attitude![4]

These commitments help keep both the frontline and management staff accountable to each other and the process. They provide an excellent accountability model for history organizations of all shapes and sizes.

How to Address Your Own Unconscious Bias So You Can Talk with Students

Keep in mind that staff communicates their discomfort by what they say and what they *do not say* during a school program. The Museum of Tolerance in Los Angeles trains staff specifically along these lines. "In the worst cases, some teachers communicate their own partisan values on the topic using biased language, skewed facts, and 'colorblind' views," Linda Blanshay, director of program development at the Museum of Tolerance, writes. "But most often, as with 'race avoidance,' teachers were relatively silent because they feared saying the wrong things."[5]

To help staff avoid expressing their unconscious biases, the Museum of Tolerance uses the following training techniques:

1. *Create a Safe Space.* Model respect for students and do not make anyone feel singled out or exposed. Practice compassionate listening. "Do not listen for the sole purpose of judging, criticizing, or analyzing. Listen only to help the other person express himself and find some relief from suffering."[6]
2. *Address "colorblind" attitudes.* Be aware of the stories that you share, especially personal ones, as students might not be connecting with them the way you expect them to. "Share only stories that create empathy for all." It is important to be self-reflective, self-aware, and to examine our own biases (implicit or explicit).[7] It is also important to address comments like "I don't see race" or "I'm teaching my students to be colorblind." Statements such as these deny the importance that our society places on race and the existence of racism in our world. These comments also devalue an important part of a student's identity. "When you are denying a student's race, you

are denying the very fabric of their being. . . . Our students and their whole selves should be celebrated and seen."[8]

3. *Recognize microaggressions and changing language.* Understand the distinctions between language that divides and language that uplifts . . . exclude dehumanizing language. . . . Auditing program language is key along with a discussion (with staff and students) of the reasons behind it. If it is the job of the docents to encourage empathy in students, they must be trained to feel and act on empathy as well.[9]

Providing staff with the tools to help them understand how to talk about the topic is critical to staff and institutional success.

Becoming Confident and Competent Discussing Race in Historical and Contemporary Contexts

Slavery and race in the United States are bound together in a narrative, the legacies of which manifest themselves directly in our contemporary society. Staff must be both familiar with this history and confident in their ability to address it with students. During a training on the histories and legacies of slavery for my colleagues, the school programs staff at the Tsongas Industrial History Center, I shared information about the connections between slavery and racism, as well as the extensive reach of slavery's economic foundation of the nation. Afterward, a colleague—a white woman in her sixties—approached me in tears. She told me that she could not believe that she had not learned any of this information before and that she felt ashamed. As uncomfortable as it is to have your colleague cry during a training, I took this as a sign of success. I moved someone to engage emotionally with historical people and events. She saw a connection between her life and the legacies of slavery.

I responded to her much like I would with students: by listening compassionately as she talked through her thoughts. I acknowledged her feelings and encouraged her to think of ways she could be a part of moving the conversation forward. She has since read several of the books I recommended and has engaged with her town's diversity committee. She now feels more prepared to talk with students about the history of slavery and its connection to the northern textile industry and more empowered to address racism in her community today.

In her 2002 study of interpretation at Historic Fort Snelling, Amy Tyson interviewed the staff about their level of confidence in talking about slavery and race as part of the story of Dred and Harriet Scott. One interpreter's comment was quite troubling:

I don't make a big deal about it if I have, you know, like, African American kids. I'm not going to go on and on about slavery. I'm going to talk about the things that were going on, what people were doing and building out here. And I may talk about the more happy role models. I might talk about George Bonga [a free Black fur trader] or Dred Scott's wife.

But we don't really have the resources and the training to really jump into race relations at all.[10]

This reply reveals a myriad of concerns, including (1) his choice not to share a complete story with all visitors; (2) reducing the history of slavery to positive stories; and (3) a complete lack of training.

This example underscores the importance of educating staff members about the historic connections between slavery and race, so they can comprehensively discuss the history and conscientiously address young visitors' concerns. Glossing over stories of struggle and terror, while substituting so-called "happy" stories, disregards the oppression enslaved Africans had to overcome to survive. It also takes the focus away from the African centeredness of the institution. One cannot talk about slavery without talking about race. Survival stories help students of all races, but most especially Black youth, see how inseparable race and chattel slavery were in the United States, and help them better understand current issues around race and racism.

When keying in on race, students are likely to make connections to race-related episodes in their lives today. This is one of the biggest fears guides and educators express: What if students bring up income disparity, segregation, police violence against Black men, or another issue they find relevance in? Brandon Dillard shared how the Monticello team prepares their staff to address these concerns:

> We provided several articles for our team to read . . . (these include articles on modern slavery and sex trafficking, how plantation museums talk about slavery, issues in Charlottesville following the white terrorist attacks in 2017, race and privilege, and how to talk to students). We held several different content [sessions] where each of [the supervisors] addressed a different aspect of the history . . . and recent events. We then moved into a Roundtable Discussion so guides could share with each other and share their thoughts on these matters.[11]

By including reading and discussion in their staff training, the Monticello staff provide space for their guides to work through concerns about the connections between slavery, race, and current events.

"What if . . ."

The most frequent questions people ask me in a workshop often start with the words "What if. . . ." Museum staff want to know how to deal with unexpected situations that may arise when talking with young people about slavery. Thus, one of the most important exercises you should do is to walk your staff through various "what if" scenarios, including how your site will deal with discussions of physical abuse, rape, and family separation. As we are all human, there is never a foolproof way to protect ourselves from the shocking things visitors (especially students) will say or do.

However, we can be prepared to calmly respond and turn the situation into a learning experience for all.

1. *What if a student giggles, or verbalizes or visually shows discomfort about talking about slavery?*[12]

   Validate the student's feelings. Assure the student it's okay to be upset or uncomfortable about slavery and that laughing is an instinctual reaction to discomfort. What happened to enslaved people in the United States was awful, and it's okay to feel compassion for them. Reassure students that they are not responsible for the past and students who identify as white should not feel responsible for slavery, and those who identify as Black don't have to be ashamed their ancestors may have been enslaved. It's important to acknowledge these feelings, but we can't get bogged down in them or else we're unable to talk/listen to each other and make positive changes. Emphasize that it is important that people talk about the institution of slavery in United States history so we can better understand its legacies and recognize the humanity of those who were enslaved.[13]

2. *What if a student (jokingly) says that slavery seemed great?*[14]

   You can ask the student, "Why do you think it was great?" They might answer "Because enslaved people got fed, clothed, housed, medical care, etc." Share with students that such replies were part of a common argument southerners/southern sympathizers made before and during the Civil War. It was based on racist beliefs that Black people were not able to take care of themselves. The idea helped white people justify a system that dehumanized Black people, one that took away their autonomy and freedom. You may want to ask the student, "How do you think it would feel to have your humanity ignored and freedoms taken away?" This question challenges the student's response in a way that causes him to think critically, rather than just shutting him down for being inappropriate.

3. *What if a student says to a white staff member, "What gives you the right to talk about slavery?"*[15]

   Answer that the history of slavery is an integral part of U.S. history and is part of our national collective narrative. Say, "As an educator here, it's my responsibility to talk about the history of slavery. It's important that we (the universal "we"/people) talk about the institution of slavery in U.S. history so that we can understand its legacies and recognize the humanity of those who were enslaved." Invite the students to share their perspectives on the institution of slavery.

4. *What if a student or teacher says they are offended by something you said?*[16]

   Apologize. If they did not specifically mention what you said that offended them (and if you can find a convenient time), ask them what it was that you said that offended them so that you can better understand their point of view.

Acknowledge that you want to learn from them so that you can do better in the future. However—*and this is important*—you must approach it differently if a historical fact was the cause of the offense. Do not apologize for historical truths that you can back up with documentation. Instead, help the student or teacher understand the origin of the historical information (present the document if you have it) and provide them with some context to help them work through their learning crisis, as they are obviously trying to integrate this new information with existing knowledge.

5. *What if some teachers tell you they do not want you to talk about slavery during a program/field trip?*[17]

   This might be particularly relevant to younger grades. It is important to let teachers know you will be sharing with the students age-appropriate content relevant to the history of slavery at the site and/or the topic of the program. It is okay to acknowledge to the teacher that talking about slavery can be uncomfortable, but it's important to share with students a complete picture of the lives of the people who lived and worked at this site, enslaved and free. Above all, don't make slavery a surprise. Make sure your website and external communications clearly define the student experience and explain the importance of talking about slavery in relevant grade-level experiences.

6. *What if a student brings up Black Lives Matter or another racially charged contemporary issue?*[18]

   Recognize the student's concerns and reinforce the connection between the concept of race and the institution of slavery.[19] Post-1865 racial issues and divides in our nation can be directly linked to the history of slavery. Even today, when we think we are more enlightened about racial issues, we live in a racialized society in which inequities are apparent everywhere. Once you've validated the student's concerns, segue back into the historical content by saying something like "That's why we are talking about slavery, so that we can understand the origins of some of these issues." This simple statement validates the student in the context of the content you are presenting.

7. *What if a student asks, "Was he [insert name of white man here] a good master?"*

   You must be clear that to be enslaved means someone owns you and decides for you nearly everything about your life. Thus, as Art Johnson, interpreter, Colonial Williamsburg notes, "There is no definition of what a good master is. If he is so good a master, why would he own people in the first place? . . . People have to get a grasp of the fact that a slave is a person who is owned."[20] In sum, trying to parse "good" and "bad" slave masters is a Sisyphean task you should avoid altogether.

How to Address Race and Inequity with Students

In the spirit of shared authority and student-centered learning, it is okay for staff to ask students, "How does this make you feel?" We want students to know their feelings are valid and important. I saw this in action during a field trip for high schoolers at the Moffatt-Ladd House.[21] Using the Portsmouth petition for freedom as the cornerstone of the program, the program starts with students viewing a clip from the 2011 film *The Help*.[22] The movie, set in Jackson, Mississippi, circa 1963, is one hundred years removed from slavery, but it portrays the relationship between African Americans in domestic service and the white people for whom they work. Keith Mascoll, the program's facilitator, used it to frame a conversation about race and identity, visibility and invisibility, empathy and discrimination. Students immediately connected with the content. Mascoll started the discussion by asking, "How did it make you feel?" Their responses included the following:

- "Sympathy for Aibileen [an African American maid] cause of how people talked about her."
- "People felt differently about [race issues]."
- "It was hard to see racism [occurring] so recently in time compared to slavery."
- "Uncomfortable because it wasn't that long ago."
- "Makes me want to do something."

Mascoll, an educator and actor who has portrayed many historically important Black men on stage, then led students through an amazing dialogue that helped them make connections between slavery, 1963 Mississippi, and the world around them today. But before he let them go any further, he made a point of telling the students this:

> You're living in an interesting time in history, and you'll shape what happens next. People will look back on your generation like they do on all generations. People have different views and that's okay. Political views don't make a difference to me. I don't judge people for their political views. I judge people on their values.[23]

This gave the students explicit permission to be open and honest, and they made deeper connections with what made them uncomfortable about the film clip, what Mascoll referred to as "tiny little insights into what it might have been like to be enslaved." Students noted the following:

- They were uncomfortable by the way the white characters in the film were comfortable voicing their racist beliefs in front of the people they were oppressing.
- The contrast between the maids' behavior in the two spaces—public and private. The maids had to close off their entire identity when they were serving and couldn't express emotions because of the threat of oppression.
- There are different types of racism and they change over time. It becomes more subtle and more of a mindset.

- White people would let slaves take care of their children and cook their food. The fact that they did not view their enslaved people as human beings is mind blowing.[24]

Mascoll asked the students to connect the dots, asking them how watching the movie clip helped to frame a conversation about the history of African Americans in Portsmouth. Their responses included, "To get us to sympathize with the characters and realize that racism happened," and "Even though the movie was set in the 1960s, we can apply the concepts to slavery and oppression of Black people throughout American history."[25]

He pulled the thread from Prince Whipple's courageous act of authoring and signing the freedom petition right through to them, telling the students this was their opportunity to make a difference and create a narrative. He challenged them to be the change they want to see and make choices about the type of person they want to be. Mascoll's skill as a facilitator helped the students to find relevance in the historical content and in today's race relations. He helped them make connections between the oppression of people because of race and oppression of people because of class—something the students in a mostly white New Hampshire school could relate to.

Mascoll's ability to relate to the students is part *je ne sais quoi* and part replicable skills, and he shared with me some of the techniques he uses to help students find relevance:

- Read the energy in the room—what's their body language saying, how are they reacting to what you say or what a classmate says—and use that to maintain or change the direction of the conversation.
- Meet the students where they are knowledge-wise and emotionally.
- Privilege every voice equally and make sure everyone who wants to has a chance to contribute.
- Assure the students the conversation is not about political beliefs; it's about what type of person you are and who you're going to be.[26]

In their post-visit surveys, student remarks demonstrated how Mascoll's message and facilitation skills helped them make emotional connections:

- "Keith talked about how he specifically acted a certain way to show the relationship between Prince and William Whipple. It showed how much he cared and how much it meant to him."
- "Keith had really moved me by saying how Prince had made a change even when he barely had a voice, and [we] can make a change too, to keep moving forward and fixing this problem."
- "Keith was talking about loving yourself and figuring out who you want to be in life at a young age, and it was incredibly inspiring."
- "Keith was talking about how although it's better, we are still the people that need to make the change. So, it's [up to] our generation to try to fix this horrible racism that still goes on today."[27]

His teaching techniques also help students make long-term connections with the content. Nearly a year after a November 2017 visit to the Moffatt-Ladd House with her One-Act Playwriting class, senior Abbye Chick shared her lasting impressions of the story of the petition for freedom:

> With current social/political climates where they are, I felt overall that learning the truth about slavery and its impact has helped to "fill in the gaps." It helped me to better understand why the social/political climates have transformed in the way that they have. History is important to me and I believe that knowing and understanding the past can lead to a better future.[28]

Students see what is happening in the world around them today and know that issues of race and identity continue to affect their lives. They have something important to say about it. We need to respect their voices and privilege their thoughts and opinions equally with ours. The techniques Mascoll used can be replicated at other institutions to talk about the connections between race and slavery. His confidence in his ability to talk about race and the way he prompted students to be introspective about the historical-contemporary connections can serve as a model for the field.

How Do We Demonstrate Respect for Our Students

The Museum of Tolerance's teaching techniques, listed above, remind educators to condition themselves to listen and be empathetic and to be accepting and respectful of what students have to say. Unconscious bias happens, so I consulted with professionals in the field for advice on how they would council educators to address contemporary race issues and the connection to slavery in a respectful manner.

Emmanuel Dabney, National Park Service, writes,

> I believe it is important to hear students out. My approach would be to engage in a dialogue with the students. "How do you feel about this?," "Have you learned of any historical events that seem to link past and present?," "What stories have you heard today that make you think this is normal/abnormal or could be changed?"[29]

From Elon Cook Lee, public historian and consultant,

> Interpreters can try breathing exercises to keep calm and think clearly as they talk their way through the situation. They can also remind students, or in my experience their teachers or chaperones, that the focus of the program is X and that these contemporary issues are part of a legacy of slavery and hundreds of years of violence against individuals and communities of color in the United States of America. But that works best if the interpreter is both well versed in the history of race in America along with current events.[30]

Ongoing Support for All Staff

A manager's job does not end when she prepares her staff with racial identity development skills, content, and dialogue facilitation techniques. It is only the beginning. In addition to ongoing skill development, you must continually support the emotional and mental health of your entire staff. Interpreting this challenging history is not easy for anyone and can sometimes be particularly difficult for African American staff, as Azie Dungey reflected when discussing portraying Caroline Branham, an enslaved woman at Mount Vernon:

> I think if we interpreters could have had the space to talk over some of these issues that are hard, it could have been good for everyone to be on the same page. . . . We as a nation still don't know how to have this [discussion]. So, it follows that interpreters don't automatically know how to have those discussions either. But interpreters could work together more—if [museum] departments could work together more—if we could all exchange our mutual knowledges and perspectives—everyone would benefit.[31]

To my white colleagues, we must trust in the concerns that our Black colleagues bring to us, and not write them off as hysterics or make-believe because they speak of something *we* have not experienced. African American staff members are categorically having different experiences from their white colleagues and it needs to be discussed and *believed*. Offering all staff members a brave space in which they can share fears and concerns provides the opportunity for them to have discussions that can elevate their knowledge, skills, and abilities.

Open discussions are not the only way to help staff, however. Colleagues have offered these additional ways to provide support for staff and co-workers who lead school programs.

Patricia Brooks, former manager of African American Initiatives at Colonial Williamsburg, notes,

> Practicing different scenarios of how to respond to various difficult situations during training is important. I would also recommend using staff meeting time to regularly discuss what actual situations staff encountered recently, how they managed it, how it felt, and open-up for discussion of other possible responses. This gives managers a chance to chime in on what is and is not appropriate. Regularly discussing this is also a way to recognize staff feelings that are triggered by doing this work and providing them support in doing this work.[32]

Emmanuel Dabney, National Park Service, advises the following:

> Stay current in the historical literature. How can you know what should be interpreted if you do not know the subject matter? Secondly, supervisors need to be engaged. They should know something about programs given. They should engage with students and educators to see what is being gained from experiencing this subject matter at the site or by offsite education programs. This includes supervisors observing and offering constructive criticism of programs.[33]

From Nicole Moore, Center for Civil and Human Rights,

Supervisors need to be able to hear the concerns of their staff members and support them in ideas of how to better reach students, or what could change in the interpretation. [They] need to listen to their staff, hear their suggestions, complaints, concerns, and ideas, and help them move forward in their interpretation.[34]

Public historian and consultant Elon Cook Lee writes,

At the Robbins House [in Concord, Massachusetts], we had an online repository for all challenging frequently asked questions with suggested responses. Supervisors should offer opportunities for interpreters to talk through challenging comments from the public with colleagues and supervisors.[35]

Inherent in this work is an acknowledgement of and respect for the weight of the emotional labor museum educators bear daily when talking about a history as challenging as slavery. Sociologist Arlie Russell Hochschild defines emotional labor as "the act of expressing socially desired emotions during service transactions. . . . Service agents [e.g., tour guides] are expected to experience and express certain feelings during service interactions [tours or school programs] . . . attempting to conform to those expectations causes certain pernicious psychological effects among the agents."[36]

Most museum professionals are taught that one of the cardinal rules of being a tour guide/educator is to keep personal emotions out of the interpretation and try not to upset the visitor, but, Nicole Moore argues, "[i]f there was ever a place where the sentiment 'the visitor is sovereign' needs to be abolished . . . this is it."[37] Slavery is an emotional history, so it is impossible to ask an educator to extricate his or her emotions of anger, guilt, resentment, defensiveness, despair, anxiety, numbness, grief, distrust, exhaustion, pride, or hope. That weight of emotion is particularly burdensome for people of African descent who interpret this history and its contemporary ramifications in American life because they cannot "clock out" of the narrative when they leave work.

Elon Cook Lee and Nicole Moore provide some context to this discussion. From Elon Cook Lee,

The legacy of slavery along with modern manifestations of white supremacy continue to have profound, but often implicit, impacts on the lives of African and African descended interpreters every minute of every day of an interpreter's life. Unlike white or non-Black interpreters of color, a Black interpreter is likely to spend a portion of each day working specifically in defense of their racial identity. We find ourselves defending the humanity and intelligence of enslaved or free Black historical figures, along with that of loved ones of African descent, our community and our own identities against offensive (often naïve) questions, comments and asides from not only visitors but also colleagues and supervisors. The challenging work of interpreting Blackness to the world around us is seemingly never ending and the majority of it goes unpaid. This can at times become overwhelming for some individuals.[38]

Nicole Moore adds,

There is a burden of an entire people's history on the shoulders of that [Black] interpreter, whether they like it or not. Being Black or of African descent and interpreting
slavery is a heavy experience that is emotionally draining as well as rewarding. You get
to tell the story of your people—and it's a collective YOUR people because for many
African Americans in this country who are descended from the enslaved, it's hard to
trace your family history past 1880. You get to essentially change the narrative from one
of oppression and submission and ignorance and everything your history books have
taught you, to showing the resilience, the hope, profound courage and achievements of
a people who officially gained recognition as citizens of the country they built with the
passage of the 14th amendment. They will endure taunts from visitors, criticism from
family and friends who may not understand why they choose to interpret slavery and the
lives of the enslaved, and they will also have to shoulder knowing the entire history of a
site (thinking plantation histories for the most part here) while their white counterparts
will often not have to learn the history of slave life on their site because they won't be
expected to learn it. It's exhausting and important all at the same time and there is
pressure to do it right.[39]

The connection between oppression of Black Americans in 1720, 1820, 1920, or 2020 is
explicit and part of the lived African American experience. A Black educator cannot shed
his or her skin color or identity before or after work. Like any person, their identity affects
their work. Supervisors need to be considerate of, and make it their mission to remember,
the fact that not every African American staff person is an expert on slavery or wants to
participate in its interpretation. They also need to make sure physical, emotional, and psychological protections are in place for Black employees because, again, they will have very
different visitor interactions than white staff. Remember that for people of African descent
interpreting slavery in third-person street clothes can be a vastly different experience than
in a third-person costume or first-person character.

Patricia Brooks writes,

This may be a story that African Americans have a special interest in telling, but that does
not mean that African Americans have a special knowledge of the historical story. African
American guides need just as much training and information to support them in telling
this story as anyone else. As a [former direct report] said, "I can empathize with this story
but even as a Black man I have never experienced anything like the experience of slavery,
so I don't know what these people felt." In other words, remember that your African
American staff members are twenty-first-century people with twenty-first-century experiences that don't give them any special insight into what it was like to be enslaved. They
may have some special insights into how the legacy of slavery still impacts us today, but
that is not the same as knowing what it was to be a slave. And many of them may be very
dedicated to telling the story but absolutely, positively DO NOT wish to portray a slave
or be responded to as though they are portraying one.[40]

Art Johnson of Colonial Williamsburg notes,

I will always have something that the average white person cannot draw upon, and that's my own experience of being Black. When I think what slaves had to go through, I can't say that I know exactly what slaves felt but I know what sometimes I feel in this world now. . . . Without a doubt, your ethnicity is bound to affect you.[41]

Keep these thoughts in mind as you examine the list below of replicable practices to support frontline staff who interpret slavery, particularly those of African descent:

- Ensure that there is qualified and experienced outside emotional help available before someone becomes overwhelmed. For instance, providing free therapy sessions for interpreters of color and making sure that time off for therapy doesn't somehow come back to penalize the interpreters who use it. Mental health contact information should be kept in a public space, like the required EEOC posters, and explained to all incoming staff and brought up again and again as upsetting incidents occur at the site or in the broader community.[42]
- The most important thing to understand is that employees who interpret this history want to have their thoughts and opinions heard and respected. These employees (and visitors who look like them) are still living in a society that defines them first by their ethnicity, and people of African descent are often perceived through the lens of systemic racism as less educated or having less to offer.[43]
- It's important to have open dialogue between supervisors and staff, "to know that everyone is still learning about each other and figuring out how to make the relationship work. They need to be able to have those honest conversations and develop a level of trust. Talk and check in with staff—ask, "How are you feeling?" It's important for supervisors to understand who they are and to be honest about what they're thinking and feeling.[44]
- Unless [the supervisor is] of African descent *and* gets out there in front of the public to do the interpretation, they can't ever know what it is like. Visitors respond differently to a white guide, a guide of color who is not African American, and an African American guide when discussing this subject. A white guide will never be asked [by a visitor], "Aren't you glad your ancestors were brought here as slaves, so you don't have to live in Africa?" Visitors are often the ones who turn the situation into something personal about the guide. Management and colleagues [should never suggest] that African American guides are too sensitive and take everything personally."[45]

Supervisors must be supportive when difficult visitors confront their staff. When receiving critical or negative feedback from visitors about a staff member, it is important to see or hear it with a critical eye. Patricia Brooks offers one such example:

Is the visitor complaining about things that are part of approved content? If not, does it sound plausible? Talk to staff to see if they recall anything unusual about how the audience responded. Keep in mind a visitor responding negatively to approved sensitive content might exaggerate in their minds what that content was—example: I received a complaint alleging that a guide held a group for ten or fifteen minutes in one space on a tour going on and on about masters raping slaves. I knew this had to be an inaccurate complaint because had the staff person held a tour for that long in one place it would be a total disruption of the tour rotation and his colleagues would have also complained about him holding up the entire tour schedule. Knowing the guide and his temperament, this was also unlikely and the logical assumption about what took place was that someone asked a question about masters raping enslaved women, the guide provided a historically accurate response, and moved on. The visitor, not liking the implication that rape was part of the story, remembered it as a long tirade.[46]

The physical and emotional stress of not being properly supported in their emotional labor can take a toll on frontline staff. Job dissatisfaction can rise and staff will burn out, leading to turnover at your site and good educators leaving the museum/historic site profession.[47] Creating an emotionally and intellectually supportive workplace is essential to maintain a healthy staff and a successful visitor experience.

Self-Care for Staff

In addition to support from supervisors and colleagues, it is important that staff find ways to take care of themselves. All staff must find ways of decompressing and centering themselves amidst this stressful work. For Black employees, this is of paramount importance due to the intersectionality of their identity and the history and legacies of slavery. During a conference session titled "This Costume Called My Skin: A Conversation with Members of the Black Interpreters Guild on Interpreting Black Life through Racial Justice Movements and the 'Whitelash,'" presenters offered some self-care suggestions for Black interpreters:

- Establish an internal balance and know what you need to do to keep yourself safe—mentally and physically.
- Know when to take risks. Learn to read your audience and decide who will be open to engaging in a learning dialogue and who might get too angry to learn.
- Fight the urge to be the "resident diversity expert." Black staff members should not have to serve as the organization's go-to people for all Black history or race questions. Encourage staff professional development so that others can become enlightened and informed.
- Set boundaries and limits for how far you are willing to go with interpreting certain narratives, especially with first-person interpretation.[48]

It is important for employees to speak up about their self-care needs. For supervisors, when an employee tells you that they need to do something in order to care for themselves, you *must* take them at their word and help address their needs.

Additionally, white colleagues need to be allies in this work. They can create a caring environment for their Black colleagues by listening and offering genuine support. Make allyship training an important part of your professional development. All staff should understand how they need to process their own concerns surrounding race and the history of slavery, whether talking with a colleague, deep breathing/meditation, journaling, or taking a long walk. Tour guides and educators need to figure out how they work best and be clear with supervisors about what they need. For example, a tour guide might need to take a five-minute meditation break between programs to clear his mind. Keith Mascoll counsels us to remember tours and school programs are a collaborative experience, and that guides should not "feel like the weight of the world is on their shoulders because they're the ones educating. We're all learning."[49]

Understanding the Intersection of Race and Gender Identity

Gender identity also plays a role in the giving and receiving of interpretation, and supervisors and staff must be aware of this.[50] As Elon Cook Lee shares, Black female staff "often find themselves being sexually harassed by both male and female visitors who may at the same time be making comments that connect the interpreter's identity to the sexual vulnerability of enslaved women. Supervisors should prepare interpreters for these possibilities and prepare all colleagues to help when problems occur."[51] Patricia Brooks encourages us to

> Openly discuss with [staff] the safeguards that you have in place to help protect staff—and put safeguards in place . . . reasonable measures that help to make staff feel comfortable and safe in any situation. For example: have rotations that don't leave people out of earshot of other staff members while they are with a group; plan evacuation procedures for emergencies; provide training that addressees strategies for what to do if you have individuals in your group that are making you feel unsafe; discuss how to gracefully end the tour prematurely, and share phrases you can use in varying types of situations to try to defuse disruptive behavior.[52]

Physical and emotional safety should be at the forefront of operational planning at historic sites that interpret the history of slavery.

In her video *Harassment and Sexual Assault of African American Historical Interpreters*, Not Your Momma's History founder Cheyney McKnight tearfully recounted her experience being sexually harassed by a male visitor while interpreting in costume at a high-profile historic site: "Usually it would be (adult men) hitting on me or touching me in some form or fashion. And sometimes saying really racist things to me such as, 'They let us pay to shoot the guns. Will they let us pay to whip the slaves?'"[53] McKnight recalled that she did not always feel safe in her work environment or supported by museum leadership. She offered the following advice for staff and supervisors to help navigate gender identity and visitor bias:

- Staff should call security and tell a manager right away when something happens.
- The administration needs to put policies into place that protect men and women from being sexually assaulted by visitors.
- The administration should provide staff with training on identifying and thwarting sexual harassment.

- If approached by an employee about an episode of sexual harassment, a supervisor should validate the employee's experiences and help them get the support they need to recover.
- Supervisors should ask staff what they need and how they, the supervisor, can help. Supervisors and administration should be honest with what help they can provide the staff. Don't over-promise and not deliver.
- Supervisors should connect Black interpreters with other Black interpreters, at your site or another site, so that they can support each other's experiences.[54]

As a white woman born in the late twentieth century, I do not know what it was like to be enslaved. I will also never know what it's like to be an African American woman. I will never have an experience like Cheney McKnight's. What I can do is listen, engender empathy, and ask how I can help. White people in positions of authority at museums and historic sites *must* be allies in the work by listening to and working with their colleagues to make the work environment supportive and fulfilling.[55] Institutions should seriously consider adding allyship workshops into staff training.

To do right by our student visitors, we must do right by our staff. An ongoing institutional commitment to training and support will make a difference in how your staff feels about themselves and their ability to do the job. Develop an institutional training plan that not only includes historical content but also race, identity, and bias awareness; working with different grade levels; situational awareness ("What ifs. . ."); being an effective ally; and how to exercise self-care. We must educate and take care of ourselves first before we can educate and take care of our visitors.

Notes

1. Rex Ellis, "Transforming Public History in the Atlantic World" (presentation, Transforming Public History in the Atlantic World, Charleston, SC, June 15, 2017).
2. Andrea Jones, "Interpreting Slavery in the Trump Era," Peak Experiences Lab, January 17, 2017; accessed February 24, 2019, http://www.peakexperiencelab.com/blog/2017/1/15/5rn1yxf1g74muws51mx3bmek0yupz7.
3. Brandon Dillard, email to the author, May 13, 2019.
4. Kristin Gallas, "Report on Values, Outcomes, and Outputs," Salem Maritime National Historic Site, unpublished, December 19, 2018.
5. Linda Blanshay, "Talking about Immigration with Children through a Social Justice Lens," in *Interpreting Immigration at Museums and Historic Sites,* ed. Dina Baily (Lanham, MD: Rowman and Littlefield, 2018), 60.
6. Dr. Hyder Zahed, "Compassionate Listening," *Huffington Post,* July 11, 2016, https://www.huffingtonpost.com/dr-hyder-zahed/compassionate-listening_b_10921036.html.
7. Blanshay, "Talking about Immigration with Children," 60–62.
8. Makeda Brome, "Do Not Be a 'Racial Identity Denier,'" EdWeek, accessed January 31, 2021, https://www.edweek.org/teaching-learning/opinion-saying-i-dont-see-color-denies-the-racial-identity-of-students/2020/02.

9. Brome, "Do Not Be a 'Racial Identity Denier.'"

10. "Enslaved African Americans and the Fight for Freedom," Minnesota Historical Society, accessed May 19, 2018, http://www.mnhs.org/fortsnelling/learn/african-americans.

11. Brandon Dillard, email to the author, May 13, 2019.

12. Developed by Kristin Gallas (project manager for education development) and Dr. Sheila Kirschbaum (director) for the Tsongas Industrial History Center at Lowell National Historical Park in Lowell, Massachusetts.

13. Definition of slavery: African chattel slavery in the United States deprived enslaved African and African-descended people of any legal rights and granted the slaveowner complete power over the Black men, women, and children, legally recognized as property. Adapted from Bryan Stevenson, "Slavery to Mass Incarceration," Equal Justice Initiative, video, accessed February 24, 2019, https://eji.org/videos/slavery-to-mass-incarceration.

14. Gallas and Kirschbaum.

15. Gallas and Kirschbaum.

16. Gallas and Kirschbaum.

17. Gallas and Kirschbaum.

18. Gallas and Kirschbaum.

19. "The permeable boundaries between slavery and freedom disappeared, dehumanizing racism became more entrenched and U.S.-based planters developed slave codes premised on racial distinctions and legal mechanisms of coercion that were modeled on Caribbean precedents." Justin Roberts, "Race and the Origins of Plantation Slavery," Oxford Research Encyclopedia, March 3, 2016; accessed February 24, 2019, http://oxfordre.com/americanhistory/view/10.1093/acrefore/9780199329175.001.0001/acrefore-9780199329175-e-268.

20. Ywone D. Edwards-Ingram, *The Art and Soul of African American Interpretation* (Williamsburg, VA: Colonial Williamsburg Foundation, 2016), 60.

21. "The Whipples," Moffatt-Ladd House and Garden, accessed May 22, 2018, http://www.moffattladd.org/explore/history.

22. Tate Taylor (dir.), *The Help* (Walt Disney Studios Motion Pictures, 2011).

23. Keith Mascoll, school program at the Moffatt-Ladd House, Portsmouth, NH, May 15, 2018.

24. Student comments during school program Moffatt-Ladd House, Portsmouth, NH, May 15, 2018.

25. Student comments during school program Moffatt-Ladd House, Portsmouth, NH, May 15, 2018.

26. Keith Mascoll, interview with the author, May 25, 2018.

27. Post-visit survey feedback, Moffatt-Ladd House, May 15, 2018.

28. Abbye Chick, email to the author, July 20, 2018.

29. Emmanuel Dabney, email to the author, May 24, 2018.

30. Elon Cook Lee, email to the author, May 25, 2018.

31. Amy M. Tyson, "'Ask a Slave' and Interpreting Race on Public History's Front Line Interview with Azie Mira Dungey," *The Public Historian* 36, no. 1 (February 2014): 60.

32. Patricia Brooks, email to the author, June 5, 2018.

33. Emmanuel Dabney, email to the author, May 24, 2018.

34. Nicole Moore, email to the author, May 21, 2018.

35. Elon Cook Lee, email to the author, May 25, 2018.

36. Arlie Russell Hochschild, quoted in Blake Ashforth and Ronald Humphrey, "Emotional Labor in Service Roles: The Influence of Identity," *The Academy of Management Review* 18, no. 1 (January 1993): 88.
37. Nicole Moore, note to the author, September 13, 2020.
38. Elon Cook Lee, email to the author, May 25, 2018.
39. Nicole Moore, email to the author, May 21, 2018.
40. Patricia Brooks, email to the author, June 5, 2018.
41. Ywone D. Edwards-Ingram, *The Art and Soul of African American Interpretation* (Williamsburg, VA: Colonial Williamsburg Foundation, 2016), 71.
42. Elon Cook Lee, email to the author, May 25, 2018.
43. Emmanuel Dabney, email to the author, May 24, 2018.
44. Keith Mascoll, interview with the author, May 25, 2018.
45. Patricia Brooks, email to the author, June 5, 2018.
46. Patricia Brooks, email to the author, June 5, 2018.
47. Ashforth and Humphrey, "Emotional Labor in Service Roles," 60.
48. Ashley Bouknight, Elon Cook Lee, Sara Daise, Nicole Moore, "The Costume Called My Skin: A Conversation with Members of the Black Interpreters Guild on Interpreting Black Life through Racial Justice Movements and the 'Whitelash'" (presentation, Transforming Public History From Charleston to the Atlantic World, Charleston, SC, June 15, 2017).
49. Keith Mascoll, interview with the author, May 25, 2018.
50. This information may not pertain to working directly with young people, but I think it is important to understanding an interpreter's complete experience, so I have included it here.
51. Elon Cook Lee, email to the author, May 25, 2018.
52. Patricia Brooks, email to the author, June 5, 2018.
53. Cheyney McKnight, *Harassment and Sexual Assault of African American Historical Interpreters*, Not Your Momma's History, video, July 10, 2018, https://www.youtube.com/watch?v=A0-bd2FkjwE.
54. McKnight, *Harassment and Sexual Assault of African American Historical Interpreters*.
55. "Being an ally doesn't necessarily mean you fully understand what it feels like to be oppressed. It means you're taking on the struggle as your own." (Guide to Allyship, accessed September 29, 2020, https://guidetoallyship.com/.)

CHAPTER 9

Engaging Teachers

"The purpose of education . . . is to create in a person the ability to look at the world for himself, to make his own decisions." —James A. Baldwin[1]

FROM ASSISTING with the development of a program to preparing students for their visit and reflecting on it back in the classroom, teachers are vital collaborators. Teachers are key stakeholders who will be more invested in the content, your site, and your story when you include them in your process from the beginning to the end. We should also consider teachers as learners, for when it comes to discussing slavery in the classroom, they need as much guidance and as many resources to talk comprehensively and conscientiously with students as our own museum staff needs.

The Wrap-Around Experience

A field trip should not stand by itself as a learning experience. Pre- and post-visit activities are integral to the onsite learning experience. In their article "How Secondary History Teachers Use and Think about Museums: Current Practices and Untapped Promise for Promoting Historical Understanding," Alan S. Marcus and associates affirm our understanding of the need for a wrap-around experience. "Multiple studies suggest that preparation for a museum visit and follow-up activities provide optimal learning experiences for students."[2] These activities bring context to and codify the learning. Pre- and post-visit lessons or activities are particularly important for a topic as fraught as slavery. While it is relatively common for teachers (who are already stretched thin) to overlook the resources we provide, the nature of the subject matter of slavery requires museums and historic sites to be proactive with teachers about these resources and to stress their importance as an essential part of the entire field trip experience.[3]

Pre-Visit Activities

Students who possess a foundation of knowledge related to the exhibit or program are more engaged in the field trip experience.[4] An institution can build that foundation with a short, simple pre-visit classroom activity. As you develop pre-visit materials, consult with your teacher-advisors about what's viable in the classroom and your state's curriculum frameworks to determine the activities that will work the best.[5] When developing pre-visit activities, consider your site's broad themes and historical context, and ask yourself the following: How can we help teachers integrate the field trip into their study of United States history or the origins of slavery as a global economic enterprise? What is the story of slavery at my site, and how does it fit into the broader context of slavery in the United States? Help teachers focus on what is most important for the visit by providing them with a "Top Five" list of things students should know before visiting your site.

For elementary and middle school students, pre-visit material might provide context for the elements of the institution of slavery your site does not cover (e.g., slavery and related concepts like racial identity, emancipation, the Middle Passage, and the Underground Railroad). For sites outside of the South, lessons might provide some myth-busting content to help students understand the presence of enslaved and free African Americans in the North, Midwest, and West.

An effective pre-visit activity should also introduce terminology to students (e.g., enslaved/slave, forced labor camp/plantation, enslaver/master, etc.) so they are familiar with the words the museum educator will use during the program. If you include your site's rationale for choosing those words, teachers will be better able to explain why you are using a different word than they do in the classroom. Also consider providing teachers with primary documents—either on the history of slavery in general or particular to your site—so students can read firsthand accounts of the lives of enslaved people.

Just as with onsite programs, pre- and post-visit activities must be age appropriate with content and pedagogy (See chapters 4 and 6.) A pre-visit activity can provide students an entrée to talking about slavery in a familiar environment (the classroom with their peers), so that when they are in a new setting with new people (your site and staff), they may be more willing to engage in conversation. Talking about slavery and race is inherently uncomfortable, so having students start the conversation at school might help them clear the hurdle of talking about this challenging history. Conversely, the classroom may not be a welcoming place for some students to share their feelings about slavery and race; therefore, the respectful environment that you provide for them may be an appreciated opportunity.

It is also good to provide teachers with specific guidance for talking with students about slavery and race. The advice provided in chapter 8 for preparing staff to talk about slavery also applies to classroom teachers. Offer teachers a set of discussion norms and dialogue prompts to help get the conversation started. For example, "How does race develop as an idea to justify slavery?" or "How do racial stereotypes linger in our culture today?" Refer to chapter 7 for additional dialogue techniques and question prompts. Other great resources include the Learning for Justice and Teaching Hard History curricula from the Southern Poverty Law Center and Talking about Race from the National Museum of African American History and Culture.[6]

Preparation can simply include an introduction to the site itself (video or images) so students are not completely surprised or disoriented by the setting. Post photographs or videos on your website to orient teachers and students to what they can expect during their visit. These visuals are particularly important to the many students who have never visited a plantation, historic site, or museum. The unknown is scary for many students and these visual and auditory resources help students feel more comfortable in a new setting. This is also particularly helpful for students on the autism spectrum. Providing teachers with pre-visit resources makes their job easier while also keying them and their students into the essence of the onsite experience.

During the Visit

It may seem counterintuitive to offer advice or guidance to teachers during their field trip, but remember that some teachers feel less than confident (even incompetent) in their ability to talk about slavery. Properly trained staff can model good teaching techniques for talking about race and slavery. Here's one example of a missed opportunity. While on a field trip to Lowell National Historical Park, a fourth-grade teacher blurted out an inappropriate statement to her class. The park ranger was sharing with students the difficulty enslaved people experienced when removing cotton seeds from cotton fibers (prior to the proliferation of the cotton gin). The ranger handed raw cotton to all the students and asked them to try to remove the seeds from the fibers, an activity that provides students a small insight into enslaved people's role in the cotton economy that drove the textile industry in Lowell. As the students reflected on the difficulty of the task, their teacher remarked, "None of you would have made very good slaves." The ranger was stunned, unsure how to respond. She segued awkwardly back to the program, a completely missed opportunity to model a conscientious teaching strategy.

A professional development session beforehand could have provided the staff member with possible responses (see chapter 8 for more on staff professional development). A situation like this requires guides to curb any misconceptions, while also not embarrassing the teacher. Statements such as "None of us will ever know what it was like to be enslaved" or, "Enslaved people did not have a choice in the type of work they were forced to do" offer a gentle correction to the teacher's statement that might not be conscientious or historically accurate.

Post-Visit Activities

A post-visit activity should help students codify their learning and find their own relevance in the content. When developing a post-visit activity, consider the messages you want to reinforce based on your program objectives. How should the students reflect on their experience? Might they respond to a person, story, object, or document they encountered during their visit? Would it be helpful for them to contextualize what they saw at your site within their understanding of the larger narrative of slavery in the United States or world?

You might develop an activity that connects people, objects, and place. "Curating the Slave Quarters," a lesson available on Mount Vernon's website, asks students to step into the role of curator to gather and analyze evidence from a variety of sources and create an interpretive plan for the Greenhouse Slave Quarters at Mount Vernon.[7] The lesson allows students to think about the possessions of the enslaved, and how having these items gave them the opportunity to actually possess something of their own. "You may not be able to call your body your own," the lesson remarks, "or your family your own, but it definitely puts a new spin on 'prized possessions.'"[8] With this lesson, students exercise their primary source analysis skills and expand on what they learned during their visit. This activity also helps them find relevance in the content, as they filter it through their existing knowledge and experience while constructing new knowledge, as a curator does, to create an interpretation of the enslaved experience.

Another option for a post-visit activity is to have students do a "Text to Text, Text to Self, Text to World." This activity prompts students to connect a document, object, building, or story to other things in their lives—other texts, objects, or stories, as well as personal experiences and events in the wider world. For example, you could have students read "Washington's Runaway Slave," an interview with Ona Judge, a woman who self-emancipated by running away from George Washington's household in Philadelphia. The article, which appeared in an 1845 edition of *The Liberator*, gives Ona's story in her own words. Students can make connections with other texts (e.g., any of Frederick Douglass's writings on freedom), with themselves (e.g., sharing Ona's desire to live her life on her own terms), and with the world (e.g., contemporary stories of immigrants fleeing their homelands for a better life in another country). This type of exercise allows students to see thematic threads running from past to present, and from people of the past to themselves.

Another post-visit lesson idea might have students make additional connections between slavery, race, and contemporary issues. They might connect your site's or community's history to contemporary issues of reparations, mass incarceration of African Americans, educational disparities, or residential segregation. Or they can examine the community in the immediate aftermath of slavery or during the height of Jim Crow or the Civil Rights Movement. They could answer questions about how and when their community responded to the *Brown vs. Board of Education* school desegregation decision, the Civil Rights Act, or the Voting Rights Act. Slavery officially ended in 1865, but its legacies are long and continue to affect the lives of all Americans. Students need to know that, and they can examine those connections in their communities through post-visit activities.

Teacher Professional Development

Teacher professional development is a key programming area for many historic sites and museums. Providing teachers with historical content and pedagogical resources is a standard part of our teacher training repertoire. However, there is much more to professional development than that. As Dana Mekler argues, focusing exclusively on the academic side of teaching means teachers "are rarely supported to develop their own emotional well-being as educators, in a way that makes it impossible for them to foster environments that cultivate empathy in their classrooms."[9] We need to balance our institutional goals for helping educators and their students with their academic, methodological, and emotional needs.

"Professional development for teachers is vital to student learning," Robin S. Grenier writes, "[and teachers] benefit from the knowledge and insights gained in self-directed activity, discourse, reflection, inquiry, and application in [museum-based professional development]."[10]

Teachers as Learners

Successful teacher professional development should not treat educators as just teachers of young minds. They are students too, and require engaging activities, historical context for new content, and the opportunity to dialogue with their colleagues. "Adult learners have assumptions, beliefs, and values that determine the way they interpret the world and their experiences," Ragland writes. "These assumptions may be challenged by people, events, changes in context, crises, or new experiences.... If this process leads to a change in assumptions, it also leads to a new way of interpreting the world, and transformation has taken place. Actions and behaviors will be changed based on the changed perspective."[11] We will be more successful when we to see teachers as students in their own right, as adult learners with specific needs and learning styles.

Just as we encourage challenging students' beliefs and assumptions, we should intellectually and emotionally challenge teachers too. A learning crisis can happen at any age and when we challenge teachers' strongly held narratives, they can feel threatened and overwhelmed, especially since they have held these beliefs and assumptions for much longer than their students. It is hard to reconcile the fact that what you have known all your life to be true is actually wrong. For those in positions of authority, who are supposed to know the material, it can be demoralizing to have to "relearn" history, so they need our support. Teachers need intellectual and emotional support around the content just like students do.

Goals for Successful Professional Development

As with any planning effort, you must have clear goals and outcomes in mind when planning teacher professional development. Goals might include building content knowledge, improving pedagogical skills, addressing social/emotional needs, establishing a community of practice, or creating lesson plans. I would recommend you focus on building teachers' skills—pedagogical, socio-emotional, facilitation—around teaching slavery. Content and context are easily gained through research and reading, but pedagogy is best learned in conversation with an expert or master teacher. Consider what skills and techniques your organization, or a partner/collaborator, can provide.

An example of an institutional goal for successful teacher professional development related to the history and legacies of slavery could be, as Grenier writes, to "[h]elp teachers acquire or develop new ways of thinking about learning, learners, and subject matter, thus constructing a professional knowledge base that will enable them to teach students in more powerful and meaningful ways" or to help "teachers do their own emotional work on the subjects of race and identity so that they are prepared to address this content with their students."[12] By outlining your goals first, you will then have clear guidelines for assembling the activities, speakers, and resources for a well-rounded experience.

As you write your professional development goals, you might think about keying into teachers' needs and motivations for attending in the first place. Reasons for attending training can vary, Grenier writes. Some teachers attend for personal motives: a love for history or a desire to learn more. Others have strictly professional motivations: to integrate the content into their classroom and/or an opportunity to share experiences with peers. Still others are attracted by the institution itself: your reputation, the design and facilitation of your programs, and the caliber of speakers.[13] Sometimes they might not even know what they need, as they might be coming because they were told by a supervisor to attend or because the topic is in next year's curriculum. To get an idea of what teachers are looking for, consider reaching out to the local school district's social studies curriculum coordinator, convene a teacher advisory group, or conduct your own survey of teachers in the area.

The bottom line is if you build their needs and motivations into your goals, you will build a program they will feel compelled to attend as it fulfills their wishes and requirements, creating a ready-made market for your program.

Developing Your Syllabus

Once you set your goals for teacher training, it is time to develop your syllabus. You might consider the types of experiences you will offer, arranging the schedule to allow time for reflection, and how much content is too much. Think carefully about who will lead the activities and sessions. Your staff may only have the expertise to talk about teaching with historic objects and documents or historical content related to your site, so consider bringing in a historian who can speak to the broader context of slavery in your region or the country. Try partnering with education professors from a local university or college, as they can provide age-appropriate guidance for lesson plan development and culturally responsive teaching. When it comes to leading discussions about race and identity, think about partnering with a dialogue facilitator from the local NAACP chapter, a sociology professor, or someone well versed in the topic. These experts can elevate the professional development experience for your audience.

Building Skills to Talk about Slavery in the Classroom

Many teachers express a lack of confidence in their ability to discuss the history and legacies of slavery with their students. Any number of factors influence this: personal feelings and beliefs, an unfamiliarity with ever-evolving scholarship around slavery, or simply a discomfort with how to talk about slavery and its present-day legacies. In a pre-workshop survey for Mount Vernon's 2017 George Washington Teacher Institute, "Slavery in Washington's World," educators self-reported a 53 percent level of comfort with slavery in the classroom (on a scale of 0–100, with 100 percent being very comfortable). In addition to expressing a lack of comfort with the subject matter, teachers also expressed that they were unprepared to address race in front of their diverse, or predominately white, classrooms. After the workshop, teachers noted the following:

- "Slavery/issues involving race are very touchy subjects, and I have always breezed the surface and moved beyond the topic as quickly as possible; however, I now feel empowered to thoroughly explain the evolution of slavery through to its abolition."

Figure 9.1. Educators attending the 2019 Monticello Teacher Institute in Charlottesville, Virginia, examine the fingerprints left in the bricks of Thomas Jefferson's home by enslaved laborers. ©Thomas Jefferson Foundation at Monticello

- "I'm a middle-aged white man. I feel almost embarrassed to speak of how men like me treated others two hundred, one hundred, and even fifty years ago. I don't think I'll ever be 100 percent confident (and don't really think anyone should be) when discussing matters of such human depravity."
- "I was very uncomfortable prior because I only looked at the inhumanity and teaching mostly African Americans, it was just tragic. . . . looking at the lives of the enslaved people through their own story was transformative."[14]

After participating in the Mount Vernon workshop, the teachers' collective confidence level rose by one-third, to 86 percent. So, what happened in that five-day time span that made such a difference? During the workshop, teachers focused on the stories of enslaved individuals, examined written records and archaeological evidence of slavery, developed lesson plans and activities to broaden understanding of slavery, and explored the challenge of teaching slavery and race in the classroom.[15] The staff at Mount Vernon brought in experts to help the teachers explore their own identities and unpack their concerns about teaching the connections between race and slavery. After engaging with more comprehensive content, individual narratives of enslaved people, and talking with professionals about techniques for discussing race in the classroom, the teachers expressed a deeper understanding of the content and more confidence in their abilities to discuss it with their students.

Pedagogical Techniques

As the Mount Vernon report noted, teachers are somewhat uncomfortable teaching this content. Therefore, teacher professional development should pay just as much attention to pedagogy as content.[16] You can help teachers gain confidence by modeling good facilitation techniques and best practices for them. Many of the techniques from previous chapters work well for teacher professional development. Engage teachers in contextualized hands-on activities, document analysis, and dialogue to provide them with opportunities to interact with the material in ways other than listening to a lecture. By offering the same types of activities to teachers as you would to students, you are also modeling good pedagogy.

Working with Primary Sources

Teachers are constantly on the lookout for grade-level appropriate primary sources that can help their students learn about the content from authentic voices. And while they know those resources are out there, they lack the time and access to, or knowledge of, archives and repositories to find them. Outside of a few popular narratives, *Twelve Years a Slave* or Frederick Douglass's autobiography, many teachers are at a loss for primary sources about slavery. Providing educators with primary sources about slavery and those who were enslaved is essential to helping teachers tell a comprehensive story of American history.[17] Moreover, it is also a great way to connect with people of the past, as primary documents are a window into the thoughts and actions of historical characters.

It is important to remember that few teachers, especially those with degrees in elementary education, have much formal training, if any, as historians. They do not know how historians work nor were they taught how to approach primary historical content in their teacher-prep programs. Keep in mind that people learn to learn as they learn.[18] We must help teachers so they can help their students. Handing a student some early nineteenth-century documents with no guidance is like giving them beakers of chemicals and expecting them to know how to do a science experiment. If we want to teach students to be historians, building their skills to read objects and documents to construct their own understanding, we need to help teachers learn how to extract meaning from documents so they can teach their students.

One activity you could do might be walking teachers through the process of thinking about a document, like a runaway advertisement or a bill of sale. You might start by having them respond to the following questions:

- Who created this primary source?
- When was it created?
- What powerful words and ideas are expressed?
- What feelings and thoughts does the primary source trigger in you?
- What questions does it raise?
- What was happening during this time period?
- What was the creator's purpose in making this primary source?
- What does the creator do to get his or her point across?
- What was this primary source's audience?
- What biases or stereotypes do you see?[19]

Modeling this or other primary source analysis techniques builds teachers' knowledge and skills. As one teacher from a Mount Vernon workshop remarked, "I have always been afraid of primary sources. I cannot say that is the case anymore [after the workshop]!!!! I am excited about the changes [to my teaching] that will happen due to the teachings we were exposed to!"[20] Another noted, "Before I attended the workshop, I tended to teach mostly only from one point of view. Now, I find myself being able to present many different points of views on issues."[21] By helping teachers build historical thinking skills you are helping them intellectually and emotionally engage with the content in a way that helps them teach the difficult content more effectively and from a wider variety of perspectives.

Building a Community of Practice

Another important component of teacher professional development is allowing time for participants to share teaching strategies and lesson ideas. You can help by developing a community of practice, one that builds on the professional development experience and extends its impact beyond their time with you. After a week-long workshop on the Civil War and Reconstruction hosted by a consortium of historic sites in Washington, DC, a teacher noted the "significance of community and conversation in their capacity to learn about history and to consider ways to improve their teaching."[22] When in communion with fellow educators, teachers gain insight, new pedagogy, and support for creating a brave and inspiring environment for students to learn about slavery.

The community of practice philosophy is also where the social element of learning comes to the fore. Just like museum professionals, teachers value networking with colleagues as they learn from each other. For teacher professional development to be successful, educators need a social environment for learning with built-in opportunities for reflection and the chance to talk with each other.[23] Take it from this teacher whom Grenier quoted:

> I was a bit disappointed that we did not have more time to have discussions. . . . Many of us were "really into" what was being taught to us during tours and sessions that we didn't conduct side conversations. . . . However, it would be beneficial to have at least a morning or afternoon, after all of the sessions, for people to develop and brainstorm implementation ideas.[24]

The communities of practice that form during professional development activities continue to influence teachers well beyond their time with you. Many teachers maintain those connections after the workshops, supporting each other, sharing lesson ideas, and seeking out new learning opportunities. This is a valuable component of teacher professional development and you would be wise to include communities of practice.

Teacher-Produced Lesson Plans

Most professional development workshops require teachers to create a product, usually a lesson plan, to obtain credit for their participation. This not only provides participants with a way to apply their new skills, but it also allows museums and historic sites to develop a generous online collection of teacher-vetted lesson plans. These lesson plans should meet your own institutional standards of language and naming conventions, as well as what you have deemed as appropriate techniques for the comprehensive and conscientious treatment of the history and legacies of slavery (e.g., "no" to role-playing; "yes" to open-ended questions, and a focus on personal stories). Teacher-created lessons and activities can also serve as examples of pre- and post-visit activities that provide a wraparound experience for student visitors.[25]

Investing time and resources in teachers—whether intellectual (contextual resources, primary documents, a pre-visit lesson) or emotional (counseling on discussing race/racism in the classroom, a community of practice)—helps exponentially in the creation of a better experience for teachers *and* students. Your institution will also benefit because teachers will see you as not just an attraction or a place to go, they will see you as *the* place to go and *the* subject matter expert. No one loses in this situation. If we approach it with a win-win-win strategy, then we all help to shape a more inclusive future for historical study.

Notes

1. James Baldwin, accessed July 18, 2020, https://everydaypower.com/james-baldwin-quotes/.
2. Alan S. Marcus, Thomas H. Levine, and Robin S. Grenier, "How Secondary History Teachers Use and Think about Museums: Current Practices and Untapped Promise for Promoting Historical Understanding," *Theory & Research in Social Education* 40, no. 1 (2012): 72.

3. More than twenty years of experience in the museum education field has taught me that it is unreasonable to expect teachers to do pre-visit activities. I get it; it hardly happens. But we can help teachers see why it is important. If they do not make use of our pre-visit lessons, we should encourage them to develop their own or contextualize the field trip in their existing curriculum.

4. John L. Pecore et al., "Formal Lessons Improve Informal Educational Experiences: The Influence of Prior Knowledge on Student Engagement," *Visitor Studies* 20 no. 1 (April 2017): 89–104.

5. I highly recommend that you compensate educators for their time and knowledge. If a financial stipend is not possible, offer them a free field trip for their class or a grant to pay for bus transportation. At the very least, you need to provide snacks during your meetings.

6. Learning for Justice (formerly Teaching Tolerance), https://www.learningforjustice.org/; National Museum of African American History and Culture, https://nmaahc.si.edu/learn/talking-about-race/topics/being-antiracist.

7. "Curating the Slave Quarters," Mount Vernon, accessed June 14, 2019, https://www.mountvernon.org/education/lesson-plans/lesson/curating-the-slave-quarters/.

8. Nicole Moore, note to the author, September 13, 2020.

9. Dana Mekler, "Educating for Empathy: Global Lessons from Schools and Social Entrepreneurs," in *Designing for Empathy: Perspectives on the Museum Experience*, ed. Elif M. Gökçiğdem (Lanham, MD: Rowman & Littlefield, 2019), 364.

10. Robin S. Grenier, "Now This Is What I Call Learning!" A Case Study of Museum-Initiated Professional Development for Teachers," *Adult Education Quarterly* 60, no. 5 (2010): 500.

11. Rachel Raglan, "Changing Secondary Teachers' Views of Teaching American History," *The History Teacher* 40, no. 2 (February 2007): 221.

12. Grenier, "Now This Is What I Call Learning!," 501.

13. Grenier, "Now This Is What I Call Learning!," 505.

14. Unpublished report of participant pre- and post-workshop surveys, "Slavery in George Washington's World," Mount Vernon, 2017.

15. "Slavery in George Washington's World," Mount Vernon, accessed March 9, 2019, https://www.mountvernon.org/education/for-teachers/teaching-institutes-professional-development/residential-programs/slavery-in-george-washingtons-world/.

16. Elisabeth Nevins, "Expanding Our Community of Practice: Professional Development in Museums," *Journal of Museum Education* 44, no. 2 (2019): 131.

17. Additional slave narratives include *Interesting Narrative of the Life of Olaudah Equiano, or Gustavus Vassa, the African*; *Life of William Grimes, the Runaway Slave, Written by Himself*; *The Confessions of Nat Turner*; *Incidents in the Life of a Slave Girl, Written by Herself* (Harriet Jacobs); *Thirty Years a Slave, and Four Years in the White House* (Elizabeth Hobbs Keckley); *Narrative of the Life and Adventures of Henry Bibb, an American Slave, Written by Himself*; and *Running a Thousand Miles for Freedom* (William and Ellen Craft). Secondary sources include *Never Caught: The Washingtons' Relentless Pursuit of Their Runaway Slave, Ona Judge*; *The Hemingses of Monticello: An American Family*; and *A Slave in the White House: Paul Jennings and the Madisons*.

18. Nevins, "Expanding Our Community," 131.

19. "Getting Started with Primary Sources," Library of Congress, accessed November 10, 2018, http://www.loc.gov/teachers/usingprimarysources/.

20. Unpublished report of participant pre- and post-workshop surveys, "Slavery in George Washington's World," Mount Vernon, 2016.
21. Grenier, "Now This Is What I Call Learning!," 508.
22. Maia Sheppard, Karen Kortecamp, Sarah Jencks, Jake Flack, and Alexandria Wood, "Connecting Theory and Practice: Using Place-Based Learning in Teacher Professional Development," *Journal of Museum Education* 44, no. 2 (2019): 190.
23. Grenier, "Now This Is What I Call Learning!," 502.
24. Grenier, "Now This Is What I Call Learning!,"
25. Some museums are moving away from the lesson-plan product (because they are overwhelmed by the number they have, and teachers find it difficult to directly implement other people's lesson plans) and are moving toward products like in-depth research on a topic/person, sets of primary documents, or teacher-curated exhibits.

Conclusion

"Nothing can stop the power of a committed and determined people to make a difference in our society."[1] —John Lewis

THIS BOOK is a call to action for the museum and historic site field. The framework herein aims to move the field forward in its collective conversation about the interpretation of slavery with young audiences—acknowledging the shortcomings of the past and acting in the present to develop a more inclusive interpretation of history. It is my hope that by engaging young audiences in dialogue about slavery and race we can move the country toward a truth and reconciliation process about slavery that results in a more equitable and just society.

Reflect on the framework laid out in the preface. Immerse yourself in the literature on race, identity, and historical trauma to figure out how they affect your work. (Re)define what successful interpretation of slavery is, so you can establish a strong foundation and direction for your work. Make sure that you engage in research that is broad and deep, finding the individual stories of the enslaved and putting them into context of the larger history of enslavement in the United States. You must ensure that your knowledge base includes age-appropriate and emotionally sound pedagogy that will build a brave space where students feel respected and cared for. When developing programs, keep a critical eye on the types of engagement and dialogue techniques you employ with young people. The use of objects, landscapes, images, documents, hands-on activities, and questions must prompt students to dig deeper—to analyze, synthesize, and question the past and present—and to find their own relevance in the content. Incumbent in telling the stories of the enslaved is creating a brave and empathetic space for student visitors, and our staff, to learn and grow. It is not enough to add the stories of enslaved people to our narratives; we must actively be anti-racists for the betterment of our community, the public history field, our colleagues, and our student visitors.[2]

This work is not just about knowing history and honing our pedagogy and interpretive skills. For white colleagues, we must acknowledge our privilege, which is based on our identity, that we bring to the discussion. It is our responsibility to start the dialogue and keep it going. We cannot place the burden on our African American colleagues, students, or community members. White privilege and racism are white people problems, and we must be part of the solution. We need to listen, learn, and make room for others at the table. If your table is crowded, build a bigger table. It is not about losing "white seats" at the table. It is about adding diverse voices so that we hear other points of view.

For African American colleagues, thank you for doing this work and honoring your ancestors. We appreciate you making room at your table and walking with us, blind spots and all, on the journey of racial healing. To those of you who embody the memory and spirit of the enslaved through first-person interpretation, your ability to breathe life into historical figures is an invaluable contribution to the field and our visitor experience.

I know that this book is a lot. It took me four years to write it. I provided dozens of examples and thousands of words of theory and pedagogy. It is too much to take in all at once, but it is easily divided into small chunks and taken in stride. But that is not an excuse to be lax about it. As Brandon Dillard notes, "It's not a choice for us, it's an imperative. We must do better." He encourages us to

> seek to do [the work] honestly and simply, with humility that we will make mistakes, with recognition that much needs to change to diversify our staff and the field overall. Memory in this country has been dominated by a wealthy white discourse, always. To change that, we have to broaden the way people remember the past at museums, with monuments, and at historic sites. There's still an awful lot of work to do, and it's work worth doing. I think its work the survival of our nation depends upon.[3]

We must do better to educate our young visitors about the history and legacies of slavery. They deserve our honesty and respect, as do the lives of the long-silenced millions.

Finally, I return to the thought that I posed at the beginning of the book. As we work toward a better present and future for all, our colleague Richard Josey of Collective Journeys asks us to consider one question: "What kind of ancestor will you be?"[4]

Notes

1. John Lewis from *Across That Bridge: Life Lessons and a Vision for Change*, Global Citizen, July 20, 2020; accessed October 23, 2020, https://www.globalcitizen.org/en/content/john-lewis-quotes/.
2. Ibram X. Kendi, *How to Be an Antiracist*, "An antiracist idea is any idea that suggests the racial groups are equals in all their apparent differences—that there is nothing right or wrong with any racial group. Antiracist ideas argue that racist policies are the cause of racial inequities." Penguin, June 9, 2020; accessed October 12, 2020, https://www.penguin.co.uk/articles/2020/june/ibram-x-kendi-definition-of-antiracist.html.
3. Brandon Dillard, email to the author, May 13, 2019.
4. Richard Josey, Collective Journeys, http://www.collectivejourneys.org, accessed December 22, 2018.

Bibliography

Interpreting Slavery maintains an online bibliography of additional resources related to interpreting the histories and legacies of slavery at http://www.interpretingslavery.com.

Brown, Kirsty, and Hilary Kennedy. "Learning through Conversation: Exploring and Extending Teacher and Children's Involvement in Classroom Talk." *School Psychology International* 32, no. 4 (August 2011).

Brown, Lovisa, Caren Gutierrez, Janine Okmin, and Susan McCullough. "Desegregating Conversations about Race and Identity in Culturally Specific Museums." *Journal of Museum Education* 42, no. 2 (May 2017).

Eichstedt, Jennifer L., and Stephen Small. *Representations of Slavery: Race and Ideology in Southern Plantation Museums.* Washington, DC: Smithsonian Institution Press, 2002.

Gallas, Kristin L., and James DeWolf Perry, eds. *Interpreting Slavery at Museums and Historic Sites.* Lanham, MD: Rowman and Littlefield, 2015.

Gökçiğdem, Elif M., ed. *Designing for Empathy: Perspectives on the Museum Experience.* Lanham, MD: Rowman & Littlefield, 2019.

Hindley, Anna Forgerson, and Julie Olsen Edwards. "Early Childhood Racial Identity—The Potential Powerful Role for Museum Programing." *Journal of Museum Education* 42, no. 1 (February 2017).

Horton, James Oliver, and Lois E. Horton. *Slavery and Public History: The Tough Stuff of American Memory.* New York: The New Press, 2006.

Katrikh, Mark. "Creating Safe(r) Spaces for Visitors and Staff in Museum Programs." *Journal of Museum Education* 43, no. 1 (2018).

Kendi, Ibram X. *How to Be an Antiracist.* New York: Random House, 2019.

Okun, Tema. *The Emperor Has No Clothes: Teaching Race and Racism to People Who Don't Want to Know.* Charlotte, NC: Information Age Publishing, Inc., 2010.

Pecore, John L., Mandy L. Kirchgessner, Melissa K. Demetrikopoulos, Laura L. Carruth, and Kyle J. Frantz. "Formal Lessons Improve Informal Educational Experiences: The Influence of Prior Knowledge on Student Engagement." *Visitor Studies* 20, no. 1 (2017).

Rose, Julia. *Interpreting Difficult History at Museums and Historic Sites.* Lanham, MD: Rowman and Littlefield, 2016.

Simon, Nina. *The Participatory Museum.* Santa Cruz, CA: Attribution-Non-Commercial, 2010.

Simon, Nina. "The Art of Relevance." June 27, 2016. http://www.artofrelevance.org/2016/06/27/introduction-unlocking-relevance/.

Sonu, Debbie. "Playing Slavery in First Grade: When 'Developmental Appropriateness' Goes Awry in the Progressive Classroom. *Multicultural Perspectives* 22, no. 2 (2020).

Tatum, Beverly Daniel. *Why Are All the Black Kids Sitting Together in the Cafeteria.* New York: Hachette Book Group, 2017.

Traces of the Trade: A Story from the Deep North. 86 min. Ebb Pod Productions, 2008, DVD.

Van Balgooy, Max, ed. *Interpreting African American History and Culture at Museums and Historic Sites*. Lanham, MD: Rowman and Littlefield, 2015.

Index

About the Author

Kristin L. Gallas has worked in museums for nearly thirty years. She facilitates workshops for museums and historic sites on developing a comprehensive and conscientious interpretation of slavery and speaks regularly at public history and museum conferences. Her clients include the National Park Service (Arlington House, National Capital Area Parks, Appomattox Court House National Historical Park, Little Rock Central High School National Historic Site, and Salem Maritime National Historic Site); George Mason's Gunston Hall Historic Philadelphia; Morven Museum and Garden; Royall House and Slave Quarters; The Trustees of Reservations; and Whitney Plantation. She served as a consultant for the exhibit "Lives Bound Together: Slavery at George Washington's Mount Vernon."

Kristin is the coeditor, with James DeWolf Perry, of *Interpreting Slavery at Museums and Historic Sites* (2015), among other publications, on best practices in the interpretation of slavery. Kristin holds a bachelor's degree in secondary history education from the University of Vermont and a master's degree in museum education from George Washington University. She led the education departments at the Montana Historical Society and the USS Constitution Museum and is currently the project manager for education development at the Tsongas Industrial History Center.

CPSIA information can be obtained
at www.ICGtesting.com
Printed in the USA
LVHW100824311021
702018LV00005B/302